"Ridiculous and sublime travel experiences."
—*San Francisco Chronicle* (Grand Prize Winner, NATJA)

"*Sand in My Bra* will light a fire under the behinds of, as the dedication states, 'all the women who sit at home or behind their desks bitching that they never get to go anywhere.'"
—*Publishers Weekly*

The Thong Also Rises
"*The Thong Also Rises* is a shoot-margarita-out-your-nose collection of travel essays stretching across the globe and into every area of embarrassment that you're thankful didn't happen to you."
—*Playgirl*

Whose Panties Are These?
"Freakin' hilarious…destructively funny stories of everything that can go wrong on the road for women, from having to buy velour panties in a very public Indian market to pondering the groundshaking question, 'Is my butt too small?' in Senegal."
—*Student Traveler Magazine*

More Sand in My Bra
"These true stories are full of bust-a-gut laughter."
—Powell's Books

What Color Is Your Jockstrap?
"Some stories are howlingly funny, and one, about a bot fly, will gross me out forever."
—Goodreads

There's No Toilet Paper on the Road Less Traveled
"Anyone who plans to travel should read this book.
And then stay home."
—Dave Barry

Last Trout in Venice:
"Traveling with Doug Lansky might result in a shortened
life expectancy…but what a way to go."
—Tony Wheeler, founder of *Lonely Planet*

Not So Funny When It Happened
"Noted travel writer Tim Cahill has collected the best
humorous travel pieces in one funny-bone volume."
—*Chicago Tribune*

Hyenas Laughed at Me and Now I Know Why
"Great for killing time waiting in the car."
—Goodreads

A Rotten Person Travels the Caribbean
"P.J. O'Rourke and Paul Theroux in a blender."
—Luis Alberto Urrea, author of *The Devil's Highway*

Fiction

Akhmed and the Atomic Matzo Balls
"This book is very sick. Highly recommended."
—J. Maarten Troost, author of *The Sex Lives of Cannibals*

WAKE UP AND
SMELL THE SHIT

HILARIOUS TRAVEL DISASTERS
MONSTROUS TOILETS
A DEMON DILDO

EDITED BY
KIRSTEN KOZA

TRAVELERS' TALES
AN IMPRINT OF SOLAS HOUSE, INC.
PALO ALTO

Travelers' Tales and Solas House are trademarks of Solas House, Inc.
2320 Bowdoin Street, Palo Alto, California 94306. www.travelerstales.com

Credits and Permissions are given starting on page 256.

Art Direction: Kimberly Nelson Coombs
Cover Photograph: © Kirsten Koza
Page Layout: Howie Severson
Production Director: Susan Brady

Library of Congress Cataloging-in-Publication Data

Wake up and smell the shit : hilarious travel disasters, monstrous toilets, and a demon dildo / edited by Kirsten Koza.
    pages cm
  ISBN 978-1-60952-109-7 (paperback)
  1. Travel--Anecdotes. 2. Travel--Humor. 3. Travelers' writings. I. Koza, Kirsten.
  G465.W358 2015
  910.402'07--dc23

                      2015014940

First Edition
Printed in the United States of America
10 9 8 7 6 5 4 3 2 1

Table of Contents

Introduction
Don't Push the Button!

Schadenfreude: (noun) delight in another's misfortune.
—Collins English Dictionary

WHETHER YOU'RE BEING MUGGED BY A MADWOMAN USING her pubic hair as a weapon (yes, this is in the book), are fleeing from maniacal baboons, or have to catch your loose stool sample in a thimble in a third-world hospital—it's never funny at the time. The beauty of travel is, like children, we stumble naively into these strange situations that don't happen in the familiar settings of our homes. This great unknown in a foreign country leaves us vulnerable to another kind of trip as well—the head trip.

I was utterly gleeful when Travelers'Tales offered me the job of compiling and editing the stories for *Wake Up and Smell the Shit*. I was in Kyrgyzstan when I started receiving the bulk of story submissions. On the wall of my hotel room was a button and beside the button was a sign that said, "Don't push the button." All I could think about was that button. What did it do? Did I have the room with the faulty room service button that delivered a deadly electric shock instead of vodka and caviar? What if I accidentally hit the button in the dark—would I wake up the next morning to find I'd nuked New York (and the magazine I write for) before being paid for my article?

At a hotel at home, I'd never have taken that head trip. I'd have called the reception desk and asked, "So what happens if I hit the mystery button?" But I couldn't work anything in my room in Bishkek—not the phone or the lock on my door. I pushed a button on the air conditioner and my room filled with cigarette smoke.

Some head trips in this volume are perfectly reasonable: a writer wakes in a hotel room in a pool of blood and has to piece together what happened, and another imagines murdering her annoying trip partner. Some head trips are just insane fun. Gary Buslik (who isn't paying me to say he is a master of this genre) has an imagination that makes him deserving of a free ticket on a one-way trip to Mars. Elizabeth Tasker (an astrophysicist who builds galaxies in her computer) will keep your plane safe if you're on her next flight, using the powers of her mind.

I disembarked my flight from Kyrgyzstan in Toronto to discover the managing editors at Travelers' Tales were filling my inbox with the most wonderful embarrassments, misadventures, and filth on planet Earth for *Wake Up and Smell the Shit*. Without thinking (the way we don't when we fire off an email), I responded to them:

> *I'm back from Kyrgyzstan. And I blame you all for not only the fact that I pooped my pants for the first time in my life but that it was so explosive that I back-sprayed the toilet seat lid behind me and Jackson Pollock-ed the rear wall of the outhouse (no hyperbole). I was so shocked when I shone my headlamp on that wall at 4:00 A.M. that I thought the vandalism of feces must have come from someone else, and I was disgusted that I hadn't noticed the state of the outhouse when I'd entered. Then I felt the wetness up the inside of my coat and all the way up my back.*

I realized the stucco of excrement that painted the interior of the outhouse was mine—it was all mine. At 4:00 A.M. I started cleaning the building with my limited supply of Kleenex Splash 'N Go! wipes and revolted myself so much that I also vomited on my bare feet and flip-flops. At 6:00, I was pretty sure the hosts at the yurt camp knew it was me who'd reeked destruction because they offered me vodka and chili peppers for breakfast.

James O'Reilly (Publisher) replied:

Kirsten, perhaps this outrageous little "tail" of yours could be deftly inserted into your own preface/intro. It is so good, and such a great example of how shit happens even to the most experienced of travelers, and with such reward—the memory, the humor. I still regale my daughters with my slabs of concrete shit in the Khumbu, back in 2002, when I had the misfortune to spend too many days sharing a tent with Larry [Executive Editor at Travelers' Tales].

Sean O'Reilly (Editor-at-Large) replied:

You want her to insert her tail into this? After hearing about what her tail is capable of I would treat her ass like Chernobyl.

Sean has a tale in this book and you'll soon all know what his tail is capable of, too, which brings me back to *schadenfreude*. I don't want bad things to happen to people, but it's a joy when a bad thing happens and they share the story afterward. The writers in this volume reveal their hugest humiliations and trip disasters. Don't feel guilt as you enjoy their horrors. It's no longer "at the time" when it wasn't funny. They're delighting in "regaling" you now.

KIRSTEN KOZA
Ontario, Canada

★

This book is dedicated to my friends.

Kap'n Cy

Amping up in Amsterdam.

TRYING TO REIGNITE THE OLD FLAME, I BRIBED MY WIFE WITH a trip to Europe. Because her family, grim-faced Aryans with the collective personality of measles, believed they were descended from a super-race of Germanic geniuses, including Wagner, Goethe, and the guy who invented beer, and further believing that the high points of human achievement were Heinz Ketchup[1] and Christmas ornaments made out of dried *schupfnudels* and *jägerschnitzels*, I thought it might excite my wife's passion to visit Amsterdam, the city that represented, in effect, the Teutonic tiki bar, where those wacky fascist partygoers almost made it under the genocidal limbo pole.

I use the term *reignite the old flame* generously, the "flame" having been one of those chemical glow sticks that you have to crack and shake to generate a cold, eerie light. In fact, my wife had not spoken to me for the prior six months because, as near as I could figure it, I had forgotten to rinse out my coffee mug before putting it in the sink. Germans fucked up the twentieth century, but they do tend to be tidy. My own people are too busy

---

[1] "Catsup!" shouted Uncle Hans, goose stepping.

controlling the world's banking system to worry about Formica stains.

In any event, it being clear that I had something to grovel for, I offered to take her to Europe, and she said, "What about my mother?"

Fortunately, old Affenpinscher Face died a few weeks before our trip date, and, just as with the Nuremberg trials, in which Hermann Goering swallowed a cyanide capsule the night before he was to be executed, saving the Allies the cost of a post-hanging reception and union musicians, I was able to secure a complete refund on my mom-in-law's airfare and hotel, said refund, as you shall see, providing me the extra cash to purchase a colossal vibrating dildo.

Our first night in Amsterdam found us, minus croaked Bavarian Mountain Hound, wandering the Old Center's picturesque cobblestone streets and quaint canals. It was the first week of December, and the gingerbread houses and ancient footbridges were twinkling with holiday lights, reflected celestially in the romantic, swan-dotted waterways. We stopped at a cozy restaurant (de Oester-bar, Leidseplein 10—pricey but pleasant) overlooking an ice rink etched by a dozen Hans Brinkers and warmed ourselves over steaming bowls of sherry-pooled lobster bisque, during which I kept thinking, *If this doesn't finally get me laid, Hitler's dream of world conquest was a total waste.*

After dinner we walked around some more, and I knew the sherry was working because when I reached for the blonde's hand she didn't scrunch her face as if she had accidentally swallowed Passover wine. Her elbow twitched, she took a half-step toward me—the wind whistled in the narrowed space between us—and cupped her mitten, but she quickly thought better of it and picked up her pace, and I fell on a patch of ice trying to catch up.

We turned a corner, and there was a sign for the Anne Frank House (Prinsengracht 267). The Dutch, keen merchants, have turned the building into a memorial museum, the second most visited site in Amsterdam, right after the Prostitution Information Center, a 15-minute stroll east (Enge Kerksteeg 3, across from the old St. Nicholas church and the Princess Juliana Basic School for children aged 4 to 12).[2]

This was not serendipitous. That afternoon, on our ride from the airport to the hotel, when our cab driver pointed out the Anne Frank House, I happened to notice, right around the corner, the neon-pulsating De Maximus Boutique, and I had a hunch it was a sex shop because its sign featured an erect penis wearing a Roman emperor's laurel wreath and wielding a four-foot-long gladiator sword. It's simple math: if a penis's sword is four feet long, the penis itself has to be, what? Of course this is the kind of dimension you absolutely would want to pulsate in neon, even in daylight. So when, tonight, we got to the Anne Frank museum ticket seller, I was about to ask for two admissions, when I suddenly grabbed my butt and said, "Uh oh."

"What?" the blonde asked, glowering.

"I have to make."

"Trust me, Germans taught these people how to install indoor plumbing."

I grimaced. "This is the real deal. I need to go back to our room for an Imodium A-D. Must have been the lobster bisque. You go ahead, I'll run there and be right back."

"How come you never think ahead? Lutherans always think ahead."

---

[2] Which is not to say that you have to walk even that far to drop in on one of the city's myriad sex shops, which, be honest, is why you're really here.

Except regarding Stalingrad. But I kept my mouth shut. Instead, to prove my intentions, I bought two tickets, gave her one, held up the other. "No way I'm going to blow four bucks." I was including the cost of the Imodium, and that seemed to satisfy her. Germans may know exactly when they're going to get diarrhea, but Jews never waste brand-name drugs.[3]

In fact, I had thought ahead. I figured my wife would shuffle through the Frank museum solemnly shaking her head, frowning ruefully, pretending to be as ticked off at her progenitors as were other visitors but secretly negating this little blip of ancestral mischief by virtue of Handel having written terrific water music, Eva Braun having gotten a whole line of small kitchen appliances named after her, and Bismarck scoring a jelly roll.

So when our guidebook (Frommer's—I recommend it) mentioned that a typical visit to the Anne Frank House lasts about an hour, I knew my beloved towhead would take every minute of it because, for one thing, when most visitors' mouths get so exhausted with frowning they need to rush into fresh air to oxygenate their facial muscles, my wife's mouth had never known any other expression but frowning and was therefore incapable of becoming exhausted and needing to rush out.

Meanwhile, while she would be milling about Otto Frank's attic, fake-sniffling contrition, I would be meandering De Maximus's aisles of kink, shopping for just the right potion, lotion, toy, or joy to assure long-overdue bedroom bliss. By my calculations—again, thinking a*head*— my life partner, having just spent an hour admiring the evil genius of her forebears, would be in a giddily horny

---

[3] My Uncle Irv once got his arm caught in a curb sewer while trying to retrieve a Flomax.

frame of mind. So, the moment she disappeared behind the bookcase, off I scrammed to the giant penis in the sky.

Don't let Holland's principal export being the Dutch date fool you. These folks know how to run a sex shop. However much you might be pissed off at them for having to dig up your tulip bulbs every fall and replant them in the spring, once you set foot in one of these cathedrals of lubricity, all is forgiven. I don't want to go into glorious specifics because there would follow such a run on Amsterdam that the entire country would sink into the Zuiderzee, causing a tidal wave that would inundate Jamaica, an island country I happen to like very much—which I promise to explain at the end, but don't turn to it yet.

De Maximus was not some sleazy, dusty, dark, sticky, rat-hole sex shop like you find in, say, Wisconsin. No sirree. It was as well lighted, organized, and—dare I say it?—spankingly clean as a Walgreens laxative aisle. It practically screamed, "We are not tight-ass Puritan Americans! We celebrate our B and D! We don't just drink bubbly on New Year's Eve—we stick it up our *achterwerks!*"

As my contact lenses defogged, I wandered the rows, pushing Try Me! buttons, feeling Lifelike! fleshy objects, and whiffing open tubes of gelatinous substances that smelled like room-service breakfast. And then I turned a corner and—*whoa!*—my eyeballs zeroed in on the most magnificent machine ever invented since the front loader. I approached it with terror and awe. It was a gigantic, multi-dialed, toggled and gauged, two-foot-long, 220-volt (with step-down transformer for the U.S.), lights-blinking, needles-pulsating, many-and-gloriously-attachmented, Frankenstein's monster of a female orgasm machine, named, with just enough machismo to underscore its lumbering good looks, Kapitein Cyclops.[4] I don't like using a lot of hyperbole in my writing, but in this case I don't know any other way of describing this monument to futtocks-penetrating brilliance. It's an injustice to call it a mere vibrator. It may as well have been sculpted from a single block of marble, a *La Pietà* of cumdom, the G-spot of the Sistine Chapel. Or, since we were, after all, in Amsterdam, a *Night Watch* of vaginal bliss. I don't know if "vaginal bliss" and "*Night Watch*" have ever been used analogously before, and I don't care. *Night Watch* was Rembrandt's greatest painting, and it has its own room in the Rijksmuseum (Stadhouderskade 42—leave yourself a whole day), and it takes up an entire wall, and it is a picture of a bunch of seriously randy guys trying to force their way into an Amsterdam sex shop.

When De Maximus's clerk gave me the price in guilders, I didn't even bother to calculate. I just handed her my wallet. She said, "It also comes in a diesel model. No problems with electric conversion, *ja*?" Kapitein Cyclops was an entire goddamn power plant. If you ran out of fuel, all you had to do was press him to your lawn, and in 15 minutes heavy crude would be gushing.

"Optional carrying case with wheels," she pointed out. "Easy on your back, *ja*?"

"I'll take it." I checked my watch. "Hurry."

She hefted it into the case, swiped my credit card—I crossed my fingers—and when it was accepted thanked me for my wise vibratory purchase.

---

[4] The Dutch naval hero Maarten van Zoot Jansse Tromp (no relation to The Donald) was affectionately nicknamed "Kapitein Cyclops" after his 1587 victory over the Spanish forces (softening the so-called Invincible Armada for its imminent defeat by Sir Francis Drake), in which van Tromp lost an eye during his decisive maneuver of wrapping his ship's bowsprit with an explosive charge and ramming it up the stern of Admiral Diego de Bobadilla's flagship, *São Filipe*, blowing the galleon's and the Catholic's aftcastles to kingdom come.

"No," I assured her. "Thank *you*."

And off we rolled, the Kapitein and I, pressing against the North Sea wind, back to the Anne Frank museum, where you-know-who was just exiting. "Where the hell were you?" she demanded. She looked down at my new suitcase. "What's up with that?"

"I have a tremendous surprise for you," I said. "Something to cheer you up after your depressing ordeal involving the sadism of the Reich."

Her arm stiffened and twitched.

"A *really, really, really big* surprise," I assured her. "A *huge, enormous* surprise. A surprise that will have you shouting my name."

"On what historical basis?"

"You won't be sorry."

"If it doesn't involve vodka, I'm already sorry."

Fortunately our hotel (Schiller Hotel, Rembrandtsplein 26-36—expensive but a Green Key winner for its environmental awareness and sustainable practices, if you give a damn, which I don't) sported a lobby bar (Café Schiller—popular and noisy), and we stopped for what I hoped would be a quick one that turned out to be an excruciatingly slow one, but nevertheless with me smirking the whole time and trying not to look at the rolling suitcase.

The blonde's eyes narrowed. "What's the matter with you?"

"I love you."

"Are you drunk?"

"Intoxicated with love."

"Forget it. I'm exhausted."

"No problemo."

"Since when?"

Our typical pillow talk. This time, though, I had her. Lutherans may think ahead, but that's only presuming they've never laid peepers on Kap'n Cy. Once I had wifey in the room and lugged that 68 pounder out of its broadside, all her thinking ahead would be as useless as the *Graf Spee* against Allied torpedo bombers.

And so upstairs we went, my sweet Frau Grendel—suspiciously, if I wasn't mistaken—insisting I walk ahead of her. I unlocked the door and waved her in.

"You go first," she said. "And no funny business."

Inside, I asked her if she wanted to slip into something comfortable—for example, the bed.

"What's wrong with you?"

"I just thought, you know—snowy night in a romantic city…"

"I already told you, I'm tired. After a certain point, it's harassment."

So I unzipped the spinner and unveiled Kapitein C.

She made a wounded-hamster sound. "What the… hell…is that?"

"Say *Hoe maakt u het* [5] to our new best friend."

She reached for the phone. "I'll show you my new best friend."

"Calling for champagne?" I asked.

"*Neun ein ein.*" [6]

Which is why we came home early without speaking to each other in any language, and why when we got back to Illinois she told me she never wanted to see my stupid face again and do myself a favor and get help. And also why, a couple of weeks later, I got a letter from her attorney, Müller.

I soon had half the money I'd worked for my whole life and hated my ex very much. I never started out wanting

---

[5] Dutch for "How do you do."

[6] German for "Nine one one."

to despise the Nazi bitch, but I see how these things work. Sometimes I would dream that she was flying back to Amsterdam for a jolly night out at the Anne Frank House, and at 30,000 feet the plane blew up, and she fell into a bubbling volcanic crater. As a veteran travel writer, I know there really are no volcanoes between Illinois and Holland, but this is how psychotic dreams work, so don't write to the publisher.

The first time I had that dream, I woke up in a cold sweat, realizing what I had just done to the 200 other, presumably innocent, airplane passengers. I got out of bed, made myself some crackers and Velveeta (I could no longer afford cheese), and decided that those other passengers were probably all newly divorced blondes who also deserved to die choking on sulfuric fumaroles. So I went back to bed and self-hypnotized myself to sleep by imagining my ex waking up in a *Twilight Zone* episode in which every women's shoe store sells at only whole-sale prices, so she goes insane and jumps off the Neiman Marcus roof but instead of splatting on Michigan Avenue, lands in Gaza wearing the gold Star of David I had bought her for her birthday and that she returned to me the next day with the note, "What the hell are you sprinkling on your matzo?"

The main point here being, not all European vacations are ideal. Sometimes they start out sherry-pooled bisque but end up flesh-dissolving magma. As an eternal optimist, though, I tend to think things usually work out for the best. For example, my cat seriously loving Velveeta.

As another example: In the divorce, I lost my house, car, IRA, dental floss, caffeine-free Diet Coke, furniture, sheets, pillows, blankets, books, wristwatch, other cat, dishes, silverware, and all my tools. I felt the way Czechoslovakia must have felt in 1938. I moved into a neighborhood that features drive-up crack houses, Meetup.com pimp movie nights, all-night slamming doors, and hallway-roaming pit bulls. And sure enough, every morning I woke up and smelled the shit. On the plus side, though, I got to keep Kapitein Cyclops, so, really, I consider it a fair tradeoff. Here's why.

One day I was watching Nancy Pelosi being interviewed on *The View* while eating Pringles. I, Gary, not Nancy, was eating Pringles. What she, Pelosi, was doing was talking without moving her face, like Jeff Dunham's Akhmed the Dead Terrorist. So I was already frightened when my phone rang, causing me to jump and launch the Pringles onto my cat, which she happens to like almost as much as Velveeta.

At first I didn't want to answer because I figured it was a collection agency, but on the outside chance it was my father calling to tell me my siblings had all suddenly died, and I was now his sole heir, I picked it up.

"Gary?" came the cheerful woman's voice.

"Never heard of him."

"You sound like him! I bet you're him!"

"I told your boss I'm doing the best I can," I lied. "We worked out a payment plan," I lied some more.

"This is Lois from O'Hare Customs! Remember me?! Last December?!"

"Customs? Lois?"

"You were returning from Amsterdam?" She lowered her pitch. "Mr. Grumpy Face."

I tried to think back on what laws I might have broken.

"I'm the short redhead with big ears."

"Lois!"

"Gary!"

"Lois!"

"I got your number off the entry doc. I hope you don't mind. I think you, um, might know why?"

Indeed I did. Yes, sirree. If she was the short redhead with big ears I was recalling correctly, she had made quite a fuss over one particular item I was bringing back to the good ol' U.S. of A. The short, big-eared Customs agent who took one gander at Kap'n Cy and, bulge-eyed, exclaimed, "Wow! He's a beaut!!"

"*That* Lois," she reminded me. "I hope I'm not calling at a bad time."

I turned off *The View*. "Matter of fact, you couldn't have timed it better. I remember you well."

"And I remember your contents!"

"Short redhead, knows how to work a zipper!"

"Cute guy with stubble beard!"

"Hate shaving!"

"Your website says you're divorced. I figure men lie all the time, but why would they lie on the Internet?"

"Very insightful."

"You wouldn't lie, right?"

"Never," I lied.

"I'm wondering if that still might be the case? Unmarried, I mean."

"The Kapitein is at the helm."

"Awesome!"

"You looked great in your uniform," I said. "Very Customsish."

"You should see me without! Amazing!"

"Double awesome!"

"Quadruple amazing!"

"You like movies?" I asked.

"Love them!"

"Me too!" I lied.

"Who wouldn't?"

"Want to go sometime?!"

"OMG!"

"Amazing!"

"I'm off Thursdays!"

"I'll check my schedule!"

"I'll give you my mobile number!"

"I'll write it down!"

And so I did, and so Lowie and I went to a movie that very Thursday and sat in the back and shared a frosty malt, stopping occasionally to sword fight with our spoons. And that weekend I reintroduced her to the captain, both of us standing at attention and saluting the heroic commander. I turned on a nightlight, plugged in the ol' skipper, and hoisted my mizzenmast.

The problem being, for all its sex-shop brilliance, Amsterdam never reckoned with Lois's own Force 12 *uitbarsting*. So that in the middle of the Kapitein azimuth-thrusting up her *achterwerks*, and her pupils tacking toward the aftcastle of her skull, the nightlight went dark, my refrigerator went silent, and the Kap'n himself stalled in a dead calm.

"Uh oh," Lowie muttered.

"Hm."

"What happened?"

"Don't know."

"Sail him back."

I shook, slapped, cajoled, and pleaded with Kap'n C., but it was not to be. He had abandoned ship. Alas, despite each man paying his own, Dutch genius had let me down.

All was eerily quiet. I got up, slipped on my robe, padded to the window and saw—"Holy crap!"

"What's the matter?" Lois exclaimed, bolting up.

"The whole neighborhood! Power out!"

She stood next to me, tilting the blinds. The crack houses had all gone *pffft*. Even the traffic lights that hadn't already been stolen were lifeless retinas. "Must have been an overloaded transformer," I guessed.

"*We* did it," she gasped. "Uh oh."

Apartment doors opened and closed. Voices in the hallway. Firearms cocking. Dogs growling.

"What do we do now?" she whispered.

"Maybe we should donate the captain to Goodwill."

She chewed her lip.

"Don't get me wrong," I said. "I love seeing you happy. In fact, I haven't been this happy myself for a long time, maybe never. It's just that right now a gesture of charity might be what's called for. Before the crackheads find out the truth and torture and kill us."

She gave me a hug and a snuggle. "Never this happy? Really, honest?"

I kissed her forehead. "Never, ever."

"Do you think they'll take it? Goodwill?"

"They'll take anything. And you know the best part? They give you a blank tax-deduction letter. You fill in your own amount!"

Under my front door I could see flashlight beams sweeping along the hallway floor. More voices and cocking pistols. A light froze on my peephole.

"Where are you going?" Lois whispered, tugging my sleeve as I slipped on my sandals.

"They're already suspicious of an English literature Ph.D. with a specialty in Shakespeare. No sense stoking the fire." So I headed to the hallway to let my good neighbors know I really was a fellow capitalist. "Stay in the bathroom," I told Lowie, so when I opened the door, the pimps and whores wouldn't spot her undressed and think that I don't respect women.

I stepped out, and a dozen flashlights and semiautomatics took the measure of my sandals, robe, and stubbled mug. And then what do you think? A second later, all the hallway lights came back on. *Woop! Power restored! Grimy bulbs aglow!* And there I was, yours truly, in robe, sandals, and hockey beard, resembling the son of God, gazing divinely up and down the corridor, lovingly, forgivingly, and as the flashlights clicked off and the muzzles lowered, I became the most heavenly neighbor that rathole had ever known. Nazareth on the alley.

They fell to their knees, the shitheads, hookers, and pit bulls, one by one, Rico and LaShawnDa and Jondro and Chlamydia, and with a gentle flick of my hand, I blessed them all, my good friends, canines, and gangbangers, and wordlessly returned to my crib.

"What happened?" Lowie asked, as I ditched my sandals and robe.

"A miracle. They woke up and smelled the shit." Whereupon we returned whence we came, sans Kapitein Cyclops, and I presented the little Customs lady with, I trust I'm not seeming immodest here, the holiest Judeo-Christian *shtupping* of her life, if she was to be believed, which I absolutely did. There is something about your neighbors believing you are omnipotent that peps a fellow up. And it's a hell of a lot cheaper than Cialis.[7]

I hope I perked my neighbors up a bit, too. Not sexually or medicinally, but existentially—that believing they lived next door to the Messiah made them feel special in a way other than, say, solitary confinement; that this, yours truly, Almighty was more *guardian* than *guard*, more *all-merciful* than *all-over-my-muthafuckin'-ass*. I like to think that at least one or two of them changed their self-destructive ways, went back to live with their parents, re-enrolled in junior high, maybe even went on to pharmacy school and became good Republicans.

The next day Lowie and I kissed the captain goodbye, packed him up nice and snug, kissed him again, and took him not to Goodwill but to the Salvation Army, where I— son of God, remember—cajoled the stoned-looking clerk

---

[7]   10mg. and 20mg. tablets, 30 bucks *apiece*. Where's Obama when you need him?

into giving us *two* blank donation letters. I drove Lois to O'Hare and gave her a hug.

Sure enough, despite my Shakespeare Ph.D., my community standing picked up. From then on, I never had to fetch my mail—it would be propped up against my newly scrubbed door, along with plates of tin foil-covered cookies. I now woke up not to the smell of shit, but of Pine-Sol and chocolate chips. The missing stairway bulbs were back, the blood stains washed off the walls, and someone had thoughtfully hammered down the protruding tack heads from the stolen hallway carpet. One afternoon I came home from work to sparkling clean windows with a note taped to one—"Whoever loved that loved not at first sight!"[8] and an unbitten corned-beef-on-rye and kosher pickle in my fridge.

Oh, yeah. My ex-wife soon married a fellow Lutheran, Ray—the Drywalling While You Wait guy whose motto was *I May Be Plastered, But I Don't Drip.* On their Las Vegas honeymoon, Ray got tangled in his flip-flops and took a header, impaling his eyeball on a margarita straw. With only one eye, and that one usually checking his toe fungus, Ray subsequently had a hard time judging the top step of his ladder (the one that says Caution, Do Not Step Here) and while practicing his line dancing on said top step fell head first into his Spackle bucket. So he retired on government disability, which suited my ex because it gave them lots of travel time. One day they returned from a Caribbean vacation and, at O'Hare Customs, happened to stand in you-know-who's line. Lois held up her finger for them to wait while she tooted me on her cell phone. When I confirmed their identity, she politely asked the lovebirds to follow her to two private rooms, where ex-linebacker

---

[8] Phebe in *As You Like It* (III, v, 82). These muthafuckas had boned up on their Bard.

agents proceeded to search their cavities. Not dental cavities. And, sure enough, between Ray's buttocks they found a Pabst Blue Ribbon beer can he had cleverly fashioned into a mini-safe crammed with—you guessed it—de aromatic weed. Ja love. Real Jamaican gold, mon—de kinda shit, whiff gonna wake you up.[9]

In the third grade, Gary Buslik was voted the kid most likely to get the shit beat out of him. These days he writes essays, short stories, and novels. His work appears often in literary and commercial magazines and anthologies and has been included in eight Best Travel Writing *editions. He is the author of the novels* The Missionary's Position *and* Akhmed and the Atomic Matzo Balls. *His essay collection* A Rotten Person Travels the Caribbean *won the 2008 ForeWord Magazine and Benjamin Franklin Book Awards for travel writing. He holds a Ph.D. from the University of Illinois at Chicago, where he now teaches Shakespeare. You can visit him at: www.garybuslik.com*

---

[9]   Not for sprinkling on his matzo, I assume.

EMMA THIEME

You Go in the Morning, I Go at Night

"Thank God I have done my ~~doody~~ duty."
—*Admiral Horatio Nelson (1708-1805)*

BEFORE *CIGANA* BECAME MY HOME, I SPENT A MONTH LOOK-ing at her. She had been left on the hard in the Rodney Bay boatyard in Saint Lucia, a 27-foot Bristol sailboat built in 1968, sitting on stilts until we were ready to splash.

Cigana wasn't mine. She belonged to my friend Chris, whom I had met just six months ago in Bar Harbor, Maine. Before Chris was my friend, he was my boss—he managed the restaurant where I had worked in the summer. Halfway through the restaurant's season, he asked me if I'd be interested in helping him deliver his boat from one Caribbean island to a more southern one. From that moment on, we were friends. Although as I stood in flip-flops on the sweltering hot cement of the yard, looking up at *Cigana*—a very small whale out of water—I realized that our friendship hadn't existed for very long. I wasn't a sailor and I didn't want to become one. I was 22 years old on a one-way ticket away from home, and this was my first big leap off North America. My goal had been to get out of Maine in January and maybe become someone I didn't yet know.

Chris and I climbed up the ladder and stepped on deck. There was a tiller at the stern and a bench for you to sit on while operating that tiller. Below was a V-berth, where Chris would sleep, and a padded bench that doubled as a table, where I would sleep. There was a gimbaled Coleman stove that would swing with the boat's movement, a VHF radio, a single cheetah-print pillow that we would rotate back and forth, and that was pretty much it.

"And this is the head," Chris said. He was standing in the single foot of space that separated his V-berth from my table-bed and pointing to a toilet that looked like an accessory you could buy from a doll magazine.

"Most American asses couldn't fit on that thing," I said.

It wasn't really the size that bothered me though; it was that we were about to become roommates in 27 feet of space. Sitting on that toilet and trying to concentrate, behind a piece of plywood, while he existed two feet away—sipping a rum punch and maybe perusing a book on nautical knots—was more humiliating than just taking a dump over the side.

"Well we could just go over the side," Chris said.

We both laughed. Then we stopped talking about it.

After a month spent sanding *Cigana's* every surface, and finishing her with black tar paint labeled only with a skull and crossbones, we launched. Our first haul was 63 nautical miles to the island of Bequia. It took 8 hours in 14-foot swells and a rainstorm, and we almost laid the boat completely over. I say "we" but we weren't really a "we"— I had no business being on that boat. For the first three hours of our journey I was passed out on Dramamine,

happily snoozing on our limited seating space while my
ears filled up with raindrops.

"Can you go below deck and make us some sandwiches?" Chris asked me when I woke up.

He had been rotating back and forth between clench-
ing the tiller and abandoning it all together to mess with
the sail. I was supposed to be holding a chart and pretending to understand it, but I had taken a nap instead.

I shook my head at the idea of making sandwiches.
Looking through that hatch, down into the lair that was
"below deck," felt like reliving my worst Ketamine experience. It was a deep, demonic alternate universe down there,
a K-hole waiting to happen. All the ingredients necessary
to make a basic ham sandwich would be right in front of
my face, and yet completely out of my grasp as a I bounced
around in an empty can just trying to reach them.

"I don't think so," I said. We went hungry.

We spent a week in Bequia. I took *Rosie*, our rowboat, out
every morning and Chris taught me how to coil a line
into a perfect circle so it looked nice on the dock.

"This will get you a job on any boat," he said, admiring
his work.

I nodded. I didn't want a job on a boat; I just wanted to
get a tan on one.

We spent so much time on shore sneaking into the
yacht club to take showers and use the bathroom, that our
head conversation hadn't been revisited. By the time we
got to Mustique, I had murdered a yellowfin tuna with a
winch handle and I knew how to read a nautical chart, but
I still hadn't used that head.

We met a captain who told us about a Norwegian family who had just passed through. They were circumnavi-
gating on a Bristol not much bigger than ours.

"And the funny thing is," the guy said. "They don't even have a head. They've just been going over the side!"

Hm, I thought.

"Hm," Chris said.

That night, when all of Mustique was sleeping, I experienced my first water birth.

"I have a confession to make," I told Chris the next morning. He was making us egg sandwiches with sides of sliced mango.

I told him about how easy it had been last night, to just climb a few steps down the rope ladder and dip my bum into the cool black water. Nobody knew, nobody was up, it was completely innocent. Plus the stars were beautiful.

"I did it this morning!" he said, launching into an opinion about "cutting out the middle man" and "the fish eat it anyway."

And so it began, our spiral into the depths of real boat life. We were drinking warm rum for breakfast; our cuticles were ripping down to our knuckles from the lack of fresh water; I had bought a drum in an effort to "remake my image"; and we were dropping deuces over the safety lines like two ships passing in the dark—Chris going in the morning while I went at night.

By the time we reached Petit Saint Vincent, water birthing had become "our thing." It was the heroine of bodily functions. It wasn't wrong because we'd both agreed to it, and it wasn't disgusting because it happened in the dark.

Then I did it in the middle of the afternoon.

We were anchored off Union Island. The water: turquoise. The sand: completely white. All of our harbor neighbors existed in their own separate universes on their own separate boats, proving that yacht life is not the same for everyone.

A group of smooth-chested Eastern Europeans oiled up to their techno music on a nearby catamaran, while their hired crew served them cold bottles of Hairoun from a cooler with ice. A French woman sat on a lounge chair on the deck of her Hinckley 38, sipping an espresso and flipping through *Vogue*—occasionally looking up to scoff at the *untz-untz* beats that were polluting her holiday from next door.

And I went for a swim and took a dump in the water. I thought it would be like it always had been—invisible and instantly out of my life. It would sink or something, float away from the harbor and into the open ocean to become another morsel in the aquatic food chain. But I was mistaken. I panicked. I splashed. There was nothing I could do. The evidence that I had gotten too comfortable with (my own version of yacht life) was staring me right in the face in broad daylight—nipping at my heels when I tried to swim away, like some kind of magnetized mutant *Water World* Chihuahua.

This wasn't my first brush with humiliation brought on by bodily functions. In the 8th grade, I peed my pants while standing directly in front of my boyfriend and then claimed I had spilled some mustard. In high school, I clogged my Spanish teacher's toilet at a Christmas party. In college, I got drunk and farted in front of the guy I was in love with, then immediately cried about it. But this, this was fucking brutal.

I swam back to the *Cigana* and fumbled for the rope ladder. Finding the first rung I assumed an unavoidable squat position to start climbing. In my peripheral vision I could see our neighbor, the French woman, staring down on me from her much larger and much more expensive ivory tower—moored just a stone's throw away from dirty, little *Cigana.*

Her stare was telling me what I already knew—I didn't belong. I was an animal, a grease stain on her respectable yachting life. The European techno music was bad, but I was worse.

I pulled my body weight up the ladder and rolled onto the deck in the typical one-leg-up-near-shoulder-exposing-bikini-clad-crotch-to-the-world fashion.

"Jesus, how many mangos have you eaten?" Chris asked, looking over my shoulder, then around the harbor. Everyone had shuttered themselves inside like a bunch of frightened hobbits. The Caribbean Sea was now contaminated, no telling when it would be safe.

I shoved Chris below deck and closed up the hatch like the rest of them, locking us in our cave to contemplate our sins. "Don't go out there," I said. "We're monsters."

An hour later, we changed harbors, but we never did change our ways.

★

Emma Thieme is a 20-something freelance writer from Maine. She's good at driving long distances and bad at folding clothes. You can find more of her writing on the Matador Network, where she works as a contributing editor. Follow her @emmacthieme.

JOHANNA GOHMANN

The Wind that Shakes the Barley

The best worst first Thanksgiving ever in Dublin.

FOR THE VERY FORTUNATE AMONG US, WHEN WE THINK OF Thanksgiving we are flooded with cinnamon-scented memories of pie, family, and turtleneck sweaters in burnt autumnal shades. At the very least, we might reminisce about throwing up green bean casserole, or drunkenly arguing with our fathers about the Iraq war.

But for me, whenever I think of our cherished "Turkey Day," I am gripped with such a cringe-inducing memory that I am left with no recourse but to slap my own forehead and sing "Jimmy Crack Corn!" at optimal volume in order to shake the embarrassment from my brain.

The year is 2010, and I have the pleasure of hosting my very first, grown-up, adult Thanksgiving since getting married. I am living in Dublin, Ireland, at the time, having been lured there by my Irish husband (never underestimate the power of multiple dimples). While cooking large game birds and hosting a dinner party would make me sweat under normal circumstances, I now have the added challenge of pulling this off in a country where asking for canned pumpkin makes the clerk stare as though you've just requested stewed penguin ovaries.

Fortunately, I have two wonderful American friends who hop a plane and head over to help me celebrate My First Thanksgiving. I then invite three Irish friends and offer to initiate them into our famous gut-buster holiday. Because I have been known to burn even Bagel Bites, and am not sure whether fennel is meat or grain, I enlist one of my American visitors to cook. This friend is fortunately skilled in the culinary arts, and she happily takes on the challenge, cooking an enormous turkey and some Stove Top that was smuggled in via her carry-on. I assist her by standing at the stove and drinking wine, offering helpful commentary on how disgusting it is that there are still feathers attached to our main course.

There are a few hiccups, such as when faced with the perplexing knobs of the Celsius oven. And then there is a brief moment of Irish panic when my husband realizes she is only cooking a mere 12 pounds of potatoes. But he races to the shop in time to pick up a few more bags, and his mini-famine fears are abated.

Soon our Irish friends arrive, ready to participate in our North American custom of gluttonously overeating poultry and gravy. The Irish usually reserve this activity for something they call "Sunday Dinner," and they are very curious to learn more about our culturally specific traditions. One Irish guest is a single lad, while the other is a married fellow who is helping along his heavily pregnant wife.

Together, we gather round our kitchen table and its borrowed card table extension: four Irish, three Americans. We settle before the plastic tablecloth, passing dishes, pouring wine, cheerfully chattering about our various customs and homelands, the American *Office* vs. Gervais, and whether or not peanut butter is the work of the gods or Lucifer himself.

As a show of embracing the true spirit of Thanksgiving (but really, more for the amusement of my American guests), I invite the Irish to share with us their national anthem. It's written in Gaelic, which sounds a bit like Elvish, and is therefore quite a lingual treat for non-Irish ears. We patiently listen to their song to Sauron, then break loudly into our own rocket-filled hymn, happy to showcase our obvious anthem superiority. *U-S-A! U-S-A!*

The Irish roll their eyes at our typical American hubris, but the tension is cut short by the Bryan Adams classic, "Summer of '69." We all belt the song in its entirety, united once more, and living proof that Adams' ode to youths having sexual intercourse in the summertime is truly the anthem of the people.

The evening rolls on, silverware is clinking, gravy and wine are guzzled, and in a moment of nervous energy that is possibly aided by my fifth glass of Syrah, I decide to toy with the Irish and their ignorance of Turkey Day. I inform them that it's a very important tradition to quiz the guests on American history, and whoever answers incorrectly must then allow a mustache of shame to be painted upon their faces with the burnt end of a wine cork. The Irish nod nervously, and then excitedly field our questions. When one of them flounders, I happily smear the cork residue across his face.

Unfortunately, my ploy quickly backfires, as I am the second to answer a question incorrectly. Howard Zinn I am not. My husband takes great delight in drawing some broad, handlebar facial hair onto my upper lip, no doubt wishing he could pop the cork into my mouth and silence me for the rest of the evening.

The meal now consumed, the Irish stare at me expectantly. *And what is phase two of this Thanksgiving affair?* Their shining blue eyes seem to ask. Unsure what to do, the table falls into silence. That's when my dear pregnant friend attempts to save the moment and turns to me with a smile. *Remember that amusing story I recently told her? Why don't I share the story with the rest of the table?*

I instantly know the story she is speaking of, and without pausing to ponder if Emily Post would endorse it as polite dinner party repartee, the words are flying from my mouth: "So my friend told me that she has a friend who performs oral sex on her husband while he's defecating."

Glasses pause in midair. Second helpings of stuffing cease. In the background it seems as if even Feist has paused midcaterwaul.

"No waaaay!"

"But why?!?"

"Is he on the toilet at the time?"

I explain that *yes*, he utilizes a toilet, and there are more howls of disgust. And skepticism. I am accused of fabricating this outlandish tale. As proof, I offer to call my source and have her verify the tale. With my wobbly wine fingers, I put my iPhone on speaker and attempt to punch in her number.

"Darling." My husband gently stills my hand. He wonders, perhaps, if this call is a bad idea? Because the source, who is my friend, is also technically my editor. And therefore my boss. Wet blanket that he is, my husband thinks it might not be in my best interests to put my boss on speakerphone at a dinner party and then ask her to recount her friend's story of scatological sex play. I, of course, am quite certain that he is wrong, and that this is a perfectly sound plan. A small wrestling match ensues, until he physically pries the phone from my fingers and proceeds to hide it.

The table has now had more time to reflect on this tale of bowl-side fellatio, and now there are many pressing questions. The ladies want to know *WHY on Earth?*—while the men are bashfully trying to explain the mechanics of the prostate. Regardless, the whole room (Irish and American) is united in the front that in no known universe would they ever want to participate in such an act—neither giving nor receiving. Not with ANYONE. We are all in agreement that the couple in question should be allowed to do as they wish in the privacy of their marital lavatory, but we also agree that there is no human alive or dead with whom we would ever consider performing such a feat. Not even for Angelina Jolie! The men nod gravely. When someone throws out to the ladies the prospect of a young Paul Newman, there is, to his credit, a small pause of consideration. But still, a resounding "No!" Not even circa *Cool Hand Luke.*

More wine is quickly opened to help wash this sordid tale from everyone's memory bank. One of the Irish guests apparently needs something a bit stronger in order to press on, and he fashions a cigarillo from some magical leprechaun herbs. He invites everyone to join him outside, and we all agree. For isn't this as our Native American friends would have wanted? This passing of the Irish peace pipe from one culture to another? We all pile out the door, leaving the pregnant Irish guest to stare at the turkey carcass and sing "The Fields of Athenry" to her stomach.

We return to the bottle-strewn table, everyone now thoroughly mellowed by the peace pipe and wine and the gallon drum of potatoes. The clock is ticking near 1:00 A.M. and the evening is winding down. Glasses of water are poured, one of my American friends excuses herself to the bathroom, and a few yawns make their way around the table. I sit back, patting my full stomach with a smug, Henry VIII-esque contentment. *The party shall go down as a success,* I think.

That is, until the evening takes a turn. A horrific, irreparable turn. In under 10 seconds, all of the good tidings and cross-cultural inroads and communion over a shared meal goes up as quickly as a puff of cigarillo smoke.

What happens is this: someone says something funny. Or maybe not even that funny. But whatever it is, it makes me break into the kind of hysterical, silent laughter that causes my body to quake uncontrollably, like I'm being electrocuted while smiling. And this, in turn, causes my body to betray me, in the ultimate bodily betrayal…

I, THE HOSTESS, interrupt the relaxed discourse of the post-Thanksgiving meal with what can only be described as thunderous flatulence—a sound so magnificently booming it is as if a Concorde is once again in flight and passing o'er head.

Did that really just happen?!? Dear God, am I awake, or in the throws of the ultimate anxiety fever dream? No. I am awake. And all around me, my dinner guests' jaws have opened in astonishment. My own husband is looking at me like I have just ripped off my face and exposed reptilian lizard flesh. The room is stunned into silence. And then, from the far end of the table, I hear my poor pregnant friend's husband turn to her in accusation: "Jesus honey, was that you?"

And at this, the suspension of time ends, and the room explodes into laughter, as my friends howl, wiping tears from their watering eyes.

Nothing in my social etiquette canon has prepared me for how to cope with a humiliation of this scale. What is the correct recourse? To blush and murmur a demure "Excuse me. Anyone for more Cool Whip?" or pull the carving knife from the greasy pan and end it all, hari-kari style? My mind reels. What would Martha Stewart do? I don't know, because I'm fairly certain Martha Stewart was born without a sphincter and would never do such a thing in the first place. No, the only reasonable solution I can think of is to slide out of my chair, slip under the table, and then proceed to crawl from the room on all fours, peels of laughter chasing me into the hallway.

Seeking solace, I crawl to the bathroom and pound on the door, where my American friend is using the facilities. "Let me in!" I whimper. "Something terrible has happened!"

My friend opens the door, while she sits upon the toilet, voiding Chardonnay. "What? What happened? Are you O.K.?"

"You won't believe it…" I moan and crawl to her. I rise before her on my knees, ready to be comforted by her soothing assurances that it was just a silly faux pas…the world is still spinning…life will carry on…

"Get out!" she cries. "Jesus, get out! It looks like you're trying to blow me!"

Dejected, I crawl backward into the hallway, and she slams the door in my face. And so, my very first Thanksgiving celebration does not end as I had hoped, with sepia-toned snapshots of me and my cashmere-clad friends chuckling over cappuccinos. Rather, the evening closes with me on all fours, outside my bathroom door, a charcoal Dali mustache scrawled upon my face with a cork.

In the other room, the laughter has not died down. In fact, it appears the party has gotten a second wind—a pun I feel almost ordered by law to utilize. Someone has started up the old global anthem again, and I faintly hear strains of Adams' raspy voice, as everyone once again sing-shouts about standing on someone's mother's porch, and thinking, as one sometimes does in life, that certain moments are simply going to last forever.

★

Johanna Gohmann has written for Salon, The Morning News, xoJane, Babble, *and* Curve, *and she is a regular contributor to* Bust *magazine. Her essays have been anthologized in* A Moveable Feast: Life-Changing Food Adventures Around the World, Joan Didion Crosses the Street, The Best Women's Travel Writing 2010, The Best Sex Writing 2010, The Best Women's Travel Writing Volume 10, *and* Every Father's Daughter.

If Pigs Could Fly

Warning: story contains a professional clown and may cause involuntary squealing.

I'M LYING ON THE WHITE SAND OF BAGA BEACH IN GOA, India, when a woman approaches me wearing a red sari and carrying a large basket of fruit on her head.

"Fruit, ma'am? Pineapple, banana?"

I've just come out of the Arabian Sea, beads of warm water slowly evaporating off my back, and I'm famished. "How much for a pineapple?" I ask her, shielding the sun from my eyes.

"Pineapple ten rupees, ma'am. Banana only two rupees. You want banana?"

"I'll have a pineapple," I say, since it's only 30 cents.

The woman bends down on one knee and deftly swoops the basket—it must weigh 40 pounds—off of her head and onto my blanket. She quickly chooses a pineapple, splits it open with a wide knife and carves the meat out of its shell. Within two minutes I'm devouring the sweetest, juiciest pineapple I've ever tasted.

I spend the rest of the afternoon reading Donna Tartt's *The Secret History* while watching an East Asian man with a ponytail do tai chi as the sky turns from a baby blue to a fiery orange and—as the sun drops behind the horizon—to the lavender-gray it will remain for the rest of the night. It's my last week in Goa, and tonight I'm heading for Arambol, a beach an hour up the coast. I'm getting a ride from a professional clown named Zou Zou, a 50-year-old New Yorker who occasionally drops into the yoga class I attend on the beach every morning. He's renting rooms in both Baga and Arambol because they cost just three dollars per night. I'm meeting Zou Zou at a bar in Anjuna, where the flea market takes place every Wednesday. Most weeks I go to buy new clothes—tie-dye t-shirts and Thai fisherman's trousers—to replace the ones that have holes from being washed too vigorously by the local washerwomen, but today I'm enjoying the quiet of Baga Beach while everyone else is haggling over lungis and silver earrings while getting stoned to the drone of Goan techno music.

At 7:00 P.M. I'm sitting on the back of a Yamaha with my backpack strapped securely across my chest as the taxi driver speeds up a dirt road to Anjuna. Fifteen minutes later, I'm eating a strange combination of fried chicken and *aloo matar*, a meal you'd only find in Goa, when I spot Zou Zou spinning in circles on the cement slab that doubles as a dance floor. He's stoned out of his mind. I'm tired of Goa's hippie travelers, the way they strut around in front of the locals wearing nothing more than G-strings (even the men), smoking hookahs day and night. I'm anxious to get to Arambol, where I plan to take a paragliding class from two British guys I met at Meat and Two Veg back in Baga—the restaurant where I eat dinner when I get tired of Indian *pomfret* and *thali*.

Three cups of chai later, Zou Zou and I mount another Yamaha and make off into the night. We catch the last ferry across the Chapora River and speed toward Arambol. When we arrive, everything is dark. Unlike in Baga and

Calangute, there are no hotels in Arambol, and the handful of restaurants that dot the beach are closed for the night. I have no place to stay and no interest in sleeping in Zou Zou's bed, so together we scour the beach for some sign of life. Behind a sugarcane hut we find three teenage boys trading stories and drinking chai and ask if they can help us out. Chattering rapidly in Marathi, they nod their heads in a bobblehead sort of way and motion for us to follow.

A short way up the beach on a patch of dirt stands a one-room wooden structure. Inside, a bed lies in one corner and a drain (the Goan equivalent of a shower) in another. The window's pane is nothing but broken shards and is covered with the tatters of what once were curtains.

"How much?" I ask the boy.

"Fifty rupees," he says.

A dollar-fifty. "I'll take it. Where do I get water?" I've learned by now that homes in remote areas like Arambol have wells instead of running water. The boy leads me to a pump several yards across the field.

"Now not working," he says. "Tomorrow O.K."

"In the morning?" I ask. "O.K. in the morning?"

He does that bobblehead thing again.

"O.K.," I say. "Thank you." There's no key to the room, but it's for just one night. I say goodnight to Zou Zou and unpack my things. The mattress, I discover, is nothing more than a double sheet with a few lumps of cotton inside. I lay my own sheet on top of it—I don't go anywhere without it—and then pile what few clothes I've brought to India—a sweater, a t-shirt and a pair of long, cotton pants—on top to create a cushion. There's no pillow, so I stretch my backpack across the head of the bed and lie down, pulling half of the sheet over me to create a human *roti* roll.

Just as I'm about to fall asleep, a firecracker goes off outside my window. I'm terrified that these boys who know

I'm alone in this unlocked room will try to sneak in and rob me, but I'm not worried about getting raped because I'm too skinny for their taste. The firecrackers continue throughout the night, and I'm relieved when the sun finally crests the horizon. I try the pump across the field, but it's still not working, so I pack my bag and make my way toward town in search of Zou Zou. I find him showering beneath a palm and ask if I can use his bathroom.

"Sure," he says. "It's right there." He points to a cement structure that looks like a bona fide outhouse. I'm impressed. I take one step up, open the door and enter. After all the pineapple, chicken and chai I had, I desperately need to go. I squat down without touching the seat, which is more of a cylinder than a seat anyway, but I find it difficult to relax. I pull a pack of tissues out of my fanny pack and line the rim with them, then sit back down. My bowels are beginning to shift when I hear a strange grunting sound between my legs. I glance down and, to my horror, there is a bulbous, hairy pig snout flaring its nostrils at my ass.

"Get out of here!" I yell at the pig. "Scram!" I can't believe he's seen my butt. I can't hold it in much longer, but I'm worried I'm going to shit on this pig, so I yell at him again to move. "Shoo!" I hiss, but rather than move his head, he opens his mouth and flaps his pointy tongue. The shit descends, the pig gobbles it up, and I quickly wipe my ass and get the hell out of there.

"Zou Zou! The pigs are eating my poop!" I yell, pointing at the swine behind the outhouse. Their snouts in a puddle of muddy water (created by my urine), they peer longingly up the hole in the back of the toilet.

Zou Zou, who's toweling himself off, laughs. "Of course they are. That's a pig toilet."

I'm astonished by his nonchalance. "You mean they're supposed to do that? What in God's name is a pig toilet?"

"It's what you see there," he says, nodding toward the outhouse. "You shit and the pigs eat it. It's a win–win situation. And it's good for the environment, too, even better than wiping your ass with your hand."

"That's totally disgusting!" I make a mental note never to eat pork in India again.

After a breakfast of scrambled eggs and toast—items you can't find in most parts of India—the owner of the restaurant draws me a map to a home three streets away, where a family has a room for rent. Zou Zou accompanies me to my destination, where I meet the lady of the house, Perpetua Hernandez. My room is simple and clean with a double bed, a cement floor, and a window overlooking the front yard, where a young girl and boy wearing nothing but t-shirts play in the dirt. At one point, the boy squats beneath the lone palm tree in the yard and defecates. No sooner does he stand up than a three-foot pig trots over and eats it. Win–win, I tell myself. Win–win.

Perpetua leads me through the main room of the house, where her husband is watching TV, to a storage room with a drain in the corner. She hands me a towel and explains that when I need a shower she'll bring me a bucket of cold water, which I'll pour over myself with a small plastic cup. I thank her and ask where the toilet is. She motions for me to follow her back through the house and out into the front yard.

In the front corner of the yard, opposite the palm tree, is a small hut, the size of a restroom stall, fashioned out of palm leaves. The door, two palm leaves tied together with palm fronds, swings open and we peer inside. On the left, against one wall, are two flagstones, designed to stand on when I squat. Below the flagstones is dirt, just like the rest of the front yard. So basically I'm expected to shit in the front yard like the children, except that I get to do it behind a palm-leaf door. I notice a small cutout at the bottom of the wall behind the bricks—presumably for the pigs.

After settling in to read for a while, my stomach begins to cramp. The eggs are not sitting well with me, and I know from several previous episodes of illness that have occurred since I arrived in India three months ago that I need to get to the bathroom fast. I dread having diarrhea in the front yard, but I have no choice. I grab several packs of tissues and stuff them into my fanny pack. Outside, I open the door to the palm stall and step inside. The door remains slightly ajar when I close it, the leaves drooping to one side, but the yard is now empty except for the pigs. I step onto the bricks and pull down my pants. There's no depression between my feet, and I'm afraid to defecate on the only shoes I brought to India, so I untie my laces, remove my Converse lowtops, and lay them to the side.

I resume my squatting position, barefoot this time, and prepare for the worst. My cramps worsen and my bowels shift. Then, right when everything's about to come out, a pig sticks his hairy snout through the hole in the wall and touches his nostrils to my ass. I jump up and scream, then curse him to leave me be. I pull up my pants, step out into the yard, and find a stick. I can't hold it much longer now, so I hurry back to the bricks and try again. This time I'm armed. When the pig approaches, I whack his nose with my stick, and he squeals in retreat. I stare up at the sky, framed by a beautiful bougainvillea, and beg: "Please God, get me though this. Please get this pig off my ass."

Just then a second pig pokes his head through the door. I whack him with my stick and, at the same time, feel whiskers on my ankles again. I hit the pig behind me while the other comes through the door, the two of them teaming up in attack. "No fair!" I yell, then make like a ninja and whip my stick around in half-circles, fighting off first one, then the other, all the while squatting on the flagstones. Suddenly my bowels loosen and shit explodes all over the ground. Dissatisfied with their runny lunch, the porcine bullies back off, leaving me to clean up the mess. Two packs of tissues later, I find Perpetua and tell her I need to take a shower. I'm embarrassed that I had diarrhea in her front yard, but there's nothing I can do about it now. After my shower, I pack up my things and go in search of another room.

Two days later, I'm standing on the edge of a cliff, about to jump off. "Don't do it," a guy named Colin says. "It's not worth it." I look back at Colin, then turn toward the ocean and step off the cliff. I drop just a couple of feet before the wind catches my sail, and I'm flying. I pull softly on my right brake and the red wing above me does a ninety-degree turn. I glide along the edge of the cliff, peering at the sunbathers below, elated to be soaring with the gulls. It's amazing up here, high above the world—so peaceful and so beautiful. This is why I came to India, I think, to get some perspective on the world. I can see for a mile in every direction, and there's not a shit-eating pig in sight.

★

Meghan Ward is a freelance writer, book editor, and blogger. She is the author of Runway, *a short memoir based on the six years she spent working as a high fashion model in Europe and Japan. Her work has appeared in* Mutha Magazine, San Francisco Magazine, 7X7 Magazine, *the* San Francisco Chronicle, *and the anthology* It's So You: 35 Women Write About Personal Expression Through Fashion and Style. *She lives in Berkeley, California, and blogs at Writerland.com. Follow her on Twitter @meghancward and on Facebook @meghanwardauthor.*

When the Empire Strikes Back

It's when you assume that nobody speaks English, that everybody speaks English.

My British friend—I will call her "Louise Hely-Hutchinson," for she is of a class that frowns on getting its names in the papers—lived inside a square doughnut. Her Kensington flat wrapped around a sunken courtyard garden that served as a light well, letting in as much sun as rainy London ever experienced. True to form, she wasn't home; she was in Barcelona until tomorrow.

"Have to run! Home soon!" she'd chirped over the phone when I'd called to tell her I was going to be in the country to present an academic paper, and then the signal crackled off. The spare keys would be sprinkled in the usual places, assuming the cat hadn't run off with them.

"Hallo, Mr. Watts," I waved to her neighbor coming up the gate, a fussy older man who regarded me as a friendly Martian.

"Back for a visit, are we?" he waved back, shifting his groceries to keep the flowers from falling out. "Come on, then, Penny," he said to the panting schnauzer trotting after his heels. "There's a good girl," he nattered absently. "Come 'round later for tea if you like."

I smiled vaguely in his general direction, as it wasn't entirely obvious he was talking to me. Amicably, he nodded as he made his way up the stairs and into the graceful building, gripping the railing with his free hand as his dog wagged her stumpy tail.

Once inside, it was a short hike down the hallway, where the final key had been tucked under the sisal mat in front of her door. A few false starts and jiggles later, I was in. Louise's three-bedroom flat had high ceilings, tall windows, and hefty architectural moldings. Those were the bones. I had no idea how they would be dressed, because she changed the décor more often than some people change their underwear.

Based on the colorful Turkish carpets, oddly shaped floor urns, and antique-ish divans scattered around the living room, it would appear that her decorator was now going for some sort of posh steampunk aesthetic. Pitching my little bag unceremoniously into the foyer, I fumbled around for the lights, kicked off my sweaty shoes and padded into to the kitchen to take stock of her supplies. Her refrigerator held its usual liquid assets: cans of Guinness stout, a formidable assortment of white wines, and an emergency bottle of Veuve Cliquot. Her cupboards held a tin of loose tea, a few snack-size boxes of cereal, a box of Carr's water crackers, a jar of Marmite, and a canister of instant coffee that I kept there for emergencies. That was the complete inventory. Miss Hely-Hutchinson did not cook, clean, or do windows.

Sighing, I fixed myself a cup of Nescafé, shuffled into the guest bedroom, and promptly collapsed into bed with my traveling clothes still on, dreaming sweet dreams of running after hairy tennis balls and eating giant marshmallows.

The following evening, Louise came tumbling home, a giddy gust of disorganized delight, shedding bags and accessories in random piles all over the living room.

"Kisses!" she demanded. "Goodness, look at your hair! I don't ever think I've seen it so long!" She threw herself dramatically onto the sofa, where for the past half-hour I'd been reading all about Hugh Grant's teeth in an ancient issue of *Tatler*.

"You weren't too stranded, were you?" she inquired formally, a holdover from years of social training, even as she squirmed around like a restless five-year-old in an attempt to achieve a comfortable position. "So sorry I couldn't be here when you arrived, but every now and then I must pretend to do work." Her tone was more gleeful than sincere. Abruptly she popped back up on her feet. "Wait, wait, wait." She began hopping around in an attempt to remove her stockings. "You must tell me everything, but I simply have to get out of these ridiculous clothes. Hang on, won't take but a second." She disappeared into her bedroom and returned a few minutes later, carrying a bottle of wine and two glasses, which she set down on the coffee table. Normal enough, except that she'd put on a pair of floppy pajamas that made her look remarkably like the Velveteen Rabbit. "Now, begin," she commanded, plopping herself back on the sofa and lighting up a cigarette.

I decided to change the subject. "So...how was Barcelona?"

Languidly, the giant rabbit sat up, uncorked the wine, poured herself a glass, and took a drag of her Dunhill as a bad-kitty expression crossed her face.

"Well...?" I prodded, because I could tell she was dying to get out the story.

"Well." Her naughty smile expanded. "Yesterday, our last night in the city, we went to a frightfully trendy new club. There was a small stage with a girl covered in whipped cream for the men, and a man in whipped cream for the women, and for a few euros you could go up and lick the stuff off their bodies. You can imagine. There was a queue around the corner for the girl. I mean, she had nothing on except whipped cream and men love that sort of thing. But no one was queuing up for the man. Bea didn't want to do it, and Sophie didn't want to do it, and somehow they decided that I ought to do it." She chewed a pinkie finger on one hand and lifted up her glass with the other, her eyes glinting merrily.

"*Eep!*" I screeched in horrified, fascinated delight, bouncing up and down on the sofa in anticipation of what was coming next. "So did you?"

"You must be joking!" She wrinkled up her nose in disgust. "I wasn't that drunk—plus you know how I loathe whipped cream." She gave me a mischievous grin. "Then that obnoxious song starts up, you know the one—*da da dum deedle deedle da da*—and everyone goes simply mad and starts dancing and nobody cares anymore. It was like watching a mindless swarm of bees returning to the hive." She took a condescending drag of her cigarette.

"That's it?"

The giant rabbit stubbed out her cigarette in a hideous bowl picked up from a souk, paused, gave me a mock-appraising look, and lit a fresh cigarette, all the while looking very thoughtful, as if she were about to lecture on "The Meaning of Socratic Sacrifice in Ancient Greece." She shifted her weight and then resumed: "Everybody is dancing, Bea and Sophie had simply vanished, and the poor boy looked bored out of his mind. I didn't want him to feel too bad, so I went up and started talking to him."

"You what?"

"I didn't think he spoke any English!"

"What did you say?"

"Something like, hullo, you are a very pretty man, and I hope you don't take it personally."

"And…?"

"He said—in English English—'I think you are the most gorgeous creature I've ever seen!' I was so startled that I almost fell off the platform right there."

"He wasn't Spanish?"

"No, he's a Brit! Turns out that he was just there on holiday and had done it on a bet. His mates promised him 300 quid if he'd stay up there for an hour. The club manager fancied his looks, so she agreed to give the regular fellow a break and let James strip for the ladies."

"How on Earth do you have a conversation with a strange man wearing nothing but whipped cream?"

She took another long drag. "It was amazing. Turns out he not only went to Oxford, same as me, but now he's a broker here in London. Believe it or not, we actually know some of the same people."

"You bonded with this man? Onstage, in an S&M club in Barcelona?

"We started snogging right there!"

My mouth fell open.

Airily, she waved her cigarette to dismiss the notion that impulsively kissing a naked stranger might possibly be anything but proper. "In no time at all, you get used to being up on stage," she said primly. "You forget that everyone in the entire room can see you." Suddenly the impish smile returned to her face. "Then out of nowhere, his mates ran up and dumped beer on his head, and, well, no more whipped cream!"

"What!"

She sighed, a starry look in her eyes. "He insisted we meet here!"

"Here?" I blinked in surprise. "As in 'London' here, or 'at your flat' here? When?"

"Tomorrow!" she squealed. "He wants to use the money he won to take me someplace nice!"

Louise hadn't been home when I'd returned to her apartment in London at 1:00 A.M. the next morning following my own confusing evening with a date that wasn't a date. Ten hours later, she was still gone when I rolled out of bed and headed for Waterloo Station to hop a train to France, but any number of reasonable scenarios could explain her absence. Most likely: after dinner, she'd stayed out dancing 'til dawn with the stranger she'd met in Spain. Less likely: she'd dumped him, or he'd dumped her and she'd gone to Bea or Lily's flat to be consoled. A call was definitely in order, but as soon as I arrived at my shabby studio rental in the 3rd arrondissement, I quickly discovered that it had no phone, and I couldn't bring myself to subscribe to a mobile service. Hoping to catch her at home, I called her late at night from the Last Phone Booth in Paris—a pristine, transparent, squared-off test tube where not even a stroke of graffiti was allowed—where I stuck my Télécarte into the port and started pushing buttons.

"Louise?" I hollered into the phone. "Where are you? I can barely hear you."

"I'm at The Cow getting a bite to eat!" she hollered back. "Sorry, the group's a bit noisy."

"What happened Saturday?"

"Such a story!" Pause. She was either taking a drag or a drink, depending on where she was in her meal. "Wait, you'll be in Paris this weekend?"

"Planning on it. Wanna come over?"

"Hang on," she ordered. In the background I could hear her asking "Ulrich" to ring the reservations line on his mobile and find out the Eurostar schedule. More shuffling noises, a muffled male voice burbling with her high-pitched tones, and then she came back on the line. "How's this: there's a late afternoon train leaving on Friday, gets in the Gare du Nord at 20:50, just in time for dinner. Does that work?"

"Sure."

"Come meet me at the station?"

"Of course. Can't wait!"

"Got to run! Kisses!" The phone clicked off.

The good thing, and the bad thing, about not having a phone is that you've got to actually see the other person if you want to find out what's going on. The main thing was that Louise had survived her evening and sounded none the worse for wear. Given the way she'd met this fellow in the first place, however, it was possible that none of the plausible scenarios I'd imagined had occurred and something completely different happened. I'd just have to wait five days to find out.

So I made reservations at the weirdest restaurant in my neighborhood: the Auberge Nicolas Flamel. Established in 1407, the alchemist's house was the oldest in Paris. Flamel claimed to have found the secret for turning lead into gold, and usually I would doubt such tales except he clearly passed on the secret to J.K. Rowling, who made billions by popping Flamel into *Harry Potter and the Philosopher's Stone*. Angels danced up the doorjambs of Flamel's house, and deeply carved Gothic lettering announced in old French: "*Icy on loge* (Lodging here)" above the near left portal, and "*Icy l'on boit et l'on mange* (Drinking and eating here)." A lengthy inscription ran across the entire façade, which ended: "…forgive the poor deceased sinners, Amen."

"What do you think?" I asked Louise, who'd arrived on schedule on the Eurostar, thrown her bags in my apartment, and rushed me out the door to get to the restaurant as quickly as possible.

"I can't understand any of it," she finally answered, scrunching up her face in bemused puzzlement, "but it certainly is old!"

Cautiously, we pushed through the door and immediately smacked into a single, off-center pier, roughly hewn out of wormwood. "Ow," we both grumbled, rubbing our injured prides, and took stock of the room.

I hadn't hit my head that hard and neither had Louise, but every line in the room was askew. The interior volume was an irregular trapezoid, and the ceiling beams had the haphazard appearance of a box of no. 2 pencils upchucked by giant beavers. It quickly became apparent why my old friend Henri had urged me to make reservations: the dining room held no more than fifteen tables, the majority of which were already occupied by experts in the fine art of speaking without sound.

Our table gave Louise an excellent view of the entire room and me a good view of a terrible contemporary painting. Off to one side, the daily menu was written neatly in cursive on a small chalkboard.

A waiter whisked forward. "Would you care to consult the wine list?" he murmured in almost inaudible tones. Handing over a thick folder, he took our orders without wincing at our French and evaporated with a polite nod. As I flipped through the pages of vintages and labels, the little detail that popped out at me was a tidbit about the building's history. Flamel had set up his *auberge* as a refuge for travelers and wayward girls.

"Wayward" was such a nice euphemism for willful women who couldn't, or wouldn't, follow the rules. I wondered if Henri had suggested this place because he knew I'd pick up on his little joke. Women who get lost easily are bound to be traveling a lot, and he was quite aware of my lousy sense of direction.

"What happened in London with Alex?" Louise resumed in English, her face eager and hopeful for good news.

"Ugh," I made a sour face. "Let's just say that the whole situation was bizarre."

Her face fell in shocked surprise, melting directly into an appropriately sympathetic configuration.

"He showed up with another woman," I added dryly, "a bitchy blonde."

The shocked look took over again.

"And," I added neutrally, as I casually sipped my water, "she went home with him."

"He did what!" Louise exclaimed, setting her glass down abruptly. "Your ex-boyfriend insists you come to dinner, shows up with another woman, and then throws you over for her?" She flung up a corresponding arm to make her point, accidentally thwacking the painting behind her head. Now the thing was not only ugly, it was crooked.

"More or less," I sighed. By now, all the emotional force had drained from the story. I just wanted to give Louise the basics and move on.

"That's terrible!" When she was indignant, her hair had a way of bristling straight up that reminded me of an angry cockatiel.

"To make a long story short," I concluded archly, "I've thrown away his phone numbers again. Goodbye. The End."

Right on cue, the wine and main dishes arrived at our table, as if to signal the end of the prologue and the beginning of the main narrative. Both dishes were simply presented, but my main interest was getting to Louise's story.

"All right, Louise," I commanded. "Enough procrastinating. You have to tell me what happened!"

She stuck an investigative fork into her scallops. "He took me to the Oak Room. Have you heard of it?" she inquired doubtfully, not really expecting an answer. "Anyhow, after the reception at the Tate, he called and asked me to meet him there. Thank god I was wearing a halfway decent dress. I popped off in a cab and got there in about 25 minutes."

"Huh," I said noncommittally, munching on a buttered slice of white potato. "Was he already there?"

Instead of replying, she tipped her head over slightly. I wondered if she was unconsciously adjusting her view to match the slope in the ceiling. "I was a bit worried," she nattered in a non-sequitur sort of way, going on about fears and hopes and the problems with Spanish cabs, eventually coming back around to the subject at hand. "You meet people in clubs, and you've had a bit much, and it's different seeing them in normal light." She righted her head momentarily. Then, cautiously, she tipped it back over again. With a sigh, she said: "He had on a smart suit, and turns out he's just as good looking with his clothes on."

"That's a reversal of the usual order of things, isn't it?"

Making a face, she ignored my little jibe. "IN THE MEANTIME," she plowed on loudly, having resolved to get out her story as quickly as possible lest she get sidetracked again, "I'd rung mutual friends to see if he really was who he said he was, that sort of thing."

"Was he?"

"Most definitely yes. Turns out he'd been living in Singapore, doing work for a Japanese firm, and had only returned back to London recently. That's why we hadn't met before."

"Any dirt?"

She shook her head. "Not married, not seeing anyone as far as Lily, Ulrich, or anyone else knew. Has the usual skeletons in the closet—the balmy uncle with a sheep fetish in Shropshire, that sort of thing, but," she beamed, "—who doesn't?"

Oh dear. Being willing to wave away pervy relatives is a good sign that she's besotted. "All right," I nudged. "You're at the restaurant. Then what?"

"We get seated right away. Everything is lovely—he's lovely, the setting's lovely, and the food's lovely. I'm positively floating through the meal."

"What did you order?"

Her expression suddenly went blank. She leaned forward as if about to speak and then abruptly sat back again. "I can't remember."

"You go to one of the best restaurants in London and you don't remember what you ate?"

She hunched over, focusing. "There were truffles in there somewhere, the mushroom kind." Her expression focused again, and then she broke out into a laugh of happy embarrassment. "That's the best I can do!" Relaxing her posture, she slid down and flopped her arms over the sides of her chair, mocking her rag-doll self, then promptly sat back up, her spine schoolgirl straight again.

The cool brunette at the next table shot her a reprimanding stare. Louise put her best upper-crust Brit face back on and stared snottily right back. The woman's face registered surprise and irritation, and then turned away.

"Better behave in here, hadn't I?" Louise whispered conspiratorially, leaning far across the table, her ears fairly wiggling with glee.

"That woman is going to go home tonight and tell every person she knows that Brits are a bunch of ill-mannered snobs," I whispered back, leaning far forward so the brunette couldn't hear me.

"Sod off, then, I say!" she giggled, doing her best imitation of a Cockney accent. It wasn't very good, worse than me trying to fake a Texan drawl.

"So, he was lovely, dinner was lovely…the point is, where were you all night?" I stage-whispered across the table.

"Flying!" she squeaked, sitting back again in her chair.

"Flying?" Her answer perplexed me. "You mean, metaphorically?"

"He has a plane!"

"He has a plane?" I repeated, in a loud incredulous voice. It was too loud, apparently, for the neighbors: this time, the patronizing brunette decided to glare icicles at me. I gave her a big, toothy, American, "Hey there, how are ya?" smile. Her face scrunched up in disgust at my unseemly lack of repentance. She turned away again, having clearly decided to pretend that we were a pair of badly trained poodles. When, to my great disappointment, she didn't attempt to bribe me with a treat, I turned my attention back to Louise.

"Well, not quite," she corrected herself. "He has a sort of timeshare arrangement with another person. They split it every other week."

"You went up in his plane?"

She nodded, and dug into her scallops.

"…after *supper*?" That was like swimming after eating: the sort of thing that was disastrous for the digestion. She knew it, I knew it; it wasn't the kind of thing worth pretending didn't happen. Because it did. All the time. In odd places. Including up in the air in a two-seater, which do not come with bathrooms.

Her head bobbed in confirmation. "It was brilliant!" she beamed, sweeping up her glass of wine and taking a big gulp for emphasis. "There's a private airfield just outside of the city. He drove us out there, and then we went up."

She looked euphoric. This man was incredibly well equipped. I wondered what he carried around in his pockets. He'd probably be able to fish out a first-aid kit, the unabridged *Oxford English Dictionary*, and a box of cherry cordials, and somehow keep it all from ruining the line of his trousers.

"Then you flew around all night?"

She shook her head. "No." Her eyes glinted merrily. "We circled around London, and then we went to Scotland. It took about three hours."

"You went to Scotland?" I repeated. The echo function in my brain refused to turn off.

"We had a wonderful trip. It was just about dawn when we started to fly over the moors. The colors were simply breathtaking. I'd never seen anything like it." She looked positively giddy.

"I can't believe you did all that on the spur of the moment!" The thing was, I did believe it. I'd known her since we were teenagers, and this wasn't even close to being her most unusual date.

She nodded, smiling blissfully like she'd just been given a basket of kittens.

"So did anything happen? You must have landed somewhere?"

"We landed in a small airfield just outside of Edinburgh. At least I think that's where we were." She didn't look like she cared. "Then we stopped off at a pub to get a bite, got refueled, turned around and came back."

"And…?"

"We did get in a bit of snogging when we got back." She chewed her pinky finger, a look of fond reminiscence crossing her face. "But that's all." She still looked amazingly happy.

I gulped down several chunks of lamb. I'd been so startled by her narrative that I'd forgotten to eat. "Let me get this straight." I took a cleansing sip of water. "He treats you to one of London's best restaurants, flies you around in his plane, whooshes you over to Scotland, and behaves like a perfect gentleman the whole time." Louise was still gnawing on her pinky. "What is this man going to do for an encore?" I stopped and thought a second. "I'm jumping the gun here. Is there going to be an encore?"

Still chewing, she nodded.

"What's it going to be? Is he taking you bungee jumping in Brazil? Getting you an audience with the Pope?"

"Actually," Louise replied sheepishly, "he and his mates are heading out to Peter's castle next weekend." She took a sip of her drink.

"He knows Peter?" Another of Louise's friends, who was now a person I sometimes sat next to at dinner parties. I shook my head in amazement at the interconnectedness of her world.

She nodded, beaming. "I told you, we know some of the same people! We would have met anyway, it just happened earlier because of Spain. The castle is leaky, drafty, and has dismal plumbing, because it's a real fourteenth-century castle. But, there will be gobs of people." Her face brightened, like she'd just had a novel idea. "You should join us!" She reached over and tugged at my sleeve. "Bea's coming too, and I think Lily wants to join us. She rather fancied one of his mates at the club in Barcelona. You really must come," she wheedled. "It will be good fun."

I hesitated. On the one hand: I had too much work to get through, and definitely the wrong wardrobe for gallivanting around a castle in the countryside. On the other hand: I could call it research, you never know what might turn up inside, and it was one place I was certain I wouldn't run into the ex-boyfriend. But—

Abruptly, the tense Parisienne at the next table turned her head and said in exasperated, accented English: "Please. Just. GO." She looked like she was ready to poke us in the eye with her fork.

Mouths agog, Louise and I both stared at her in astonishment, as much for the fact that she spoke English as for the fact that she'd gotten so fed up with us that she'd lost all sense of decorum.

"Beg pardon?" Louise retorted in coldly polite tones, her hair bristling up dangerously.

"Go," the brunette repeated darkly. "Why are you here?"

Thunderclouds were gathering over Louise's head. She was about to go all Lady of the Manor on this woman, and it was not going to be pretty.

Throwing her napkin down on her plate, the French-woman pushed back her chair and stood up in one sudden move. The girl fight was about to begin. Around us, polished heads were turning, supercilious eyebrows were raising, pursed lips were silently clucking. A dinner fork is not for stabbing fellow patrons. How perfectly gauche! If you really cannot restrain yourself, please use a napkin and a steak knife. She glared at both of us, her face a grim mask. "Never!" she exclaimed in thick French accent. "Never turn down an invitation to a castle!" She wagged a long finger at me as her eyes darted to the empty chair across from her, which suddenly transformed into a horror story.

Tossing her head back, she summoned the cringing waiter with an imperious hand. With a barely disguised expression of relief, he darted forward with her bill in one hand and the credit card reader in the other. With a swipe and a sniff, she paid for her meal, and swanned out the door without a backward glance.

The room watched her depart, then, with a collective shrug, resumed dining as usual.

"Well then," Louise said, taking a sip of water as we pondered her odd speech while trying to ignore the waiter who'd moved in to clear the abandoned table. "You heard her: 'Never turn down an invitation to a castle'!"

I smiled weakly. "That sounds like a euphemism...."

"...for an adventure with naked men!" Louise squeaked, laughing from deep within her belly. "So you're coming. It's settled."

Except it wasn't.

.....*ggggrrrrrp*.

"Don't look at me," I said airily. To my great glee, this time the gastric burbles were coming from Louise, who looked utterly mortified by the sound of seafood being badly digested.

....*bloooop*!

She threw me an anguished glance. "Where...?" she began.

Smoothly, the waiter, still brushing crumbs off the table-cloth, leaned forward slightly and murmured discreetly in proper British tones, "...the W/C is to the back," as he continued whisking crumbs with an expression so impassive that I wasn't sure he'd actually said anything. Straightening up, he headed back to the kitchen, but not before turning his head ever so slightly and dropping one eyelid in a perfectly executed wink.

With an equally bland expression, Louise winked back.

A secret code reminding me that it really is true: no matter where you go, everybody speaks English.

★

Paula Young Lee is a faculty Fellow at the Center for Animals and Public Policy at Tufts University and the author of several books, including Deer Hunting in Paris: A Memoir of God, Guns, and Game Meat*, winner of the 2014 Lowell Thomas Travel Book Award from the Society of American Travel Writers.*

BETH MERCER

Costa Rican Red and a Golden Shower

Endless Summer *meets Freddy Krueger on*
The Beach.

As my eyes begin to focus, all I can see is red: fuzzy, slippery, shiny, redness. What is it? Where am I? What the? Oh, no! It all goes black. My eyes once again open to red but this time there are patches of white. Hard, cold, white, mixed in with all the red and then bang, darkness. What the hell is going on? My head hurts, my face is in agony, and I can't see clearly. I am cold. Where am I? I'm not at work—this isn't a film set. This is real. And why do my teeth feel like they are about to snap off? Why am I naked, prone on a bathroom floor? I realize I've been trying to push myself upright but have been passing out before I can get into a seated position. In the process I've been repeatedly smashing my face into the tile floor. My God, the red I see through the fog is blood. My blood. Massive amounts of it are gushing from my flattened nose and my ripped lip. Are my teeth still there? I collapse, slamming my face into the crimson-soaked floor once again. Was it a robbery? Some kind of violent attack? Maybe home invaders?

I'd arrived the day before in the town of Nosara, Costa Rica, with the intention of spending three glorious weeks surfing, sunning, running, and writing. There was a storm off the coast, bringing in a huge swell accompanied by enormous crashing waves. This was fantastic for the local boys but not so fantastic for the aspiring, over-40 surfer chick. I rented a board from a local dude named Alejandro who had the biggest mass of dreadlocks this side of Jamaica. He spent the day catching wave after wave and watching me get hammered in the thundering surf. I was a pathetic-looking creature when I returned to his rental hut at dusk with my board trailing behind me. Alejandro and his cute young surfer buddy Marco took pity on me, offering up a beer and a reefer the size of my head. I took the beer but abstained from the weed.

As we swung in hammocks, drinking Imperial and listening to Bob Marley, Alejandro and Marco smoked and pontificated about the sea, the waves, and the need to be one with the water while surfing. That was exactly what I came all this way to do—become one with the waves. Well, that and to be able to stand up on my board long enough to get a ride or two in. As the sun began to set, Marco mentioned they were going out to a little known point break down the coast the next morning. Alejandro figured it would be perfect for me. With my liquid courage flowing, I arranged to meet them at dawn the next day.

We drove about two hours down the wild coast on a bumpy, dirt track. It was the perfect morning. The boys were lovely, the conversation easy, fun, and interesting. As we rounded the last corner, a small deserted beach stretched before us. Not a soul in sight. No yoga-posing girls, no bongo-playing hippies, and no families with screaming children, just the three of us, miles from the tourist hub of Nosara. This was turning out to be my fantasy vacation.

The break looked fantastic. The waves were the perfect size and distance apart and the paddle out reasonable enough even for me. With confidence and excitement I followed the boys into the crystal-clear water. Just as the waves lapped my knees, I felt a little pinch on the second toe of my right foot. A crab perhaps? I pulled my foot out of the surf and looked at my toe. "I think I've been bitten by a crab." Blood was pouring out of it into the water. I called to Alejandro, "Hey, if I am bleeding do I need to worry about shar…" Searing pain shot up my leg. It was on fire. I must have yelled because the two men were at my side in a second pulling me out of the water.

"¡No, no, no es crab, es la raya, la raya!" Marco yelled.

"What? What the hell?" I had no idea what he was saying. All I knew was the pain in my leg was intolerable.

Marco continued repeating "la raya, la raya" in an increasingly loud voice as if that would help me understand the words of a language I didn't speak. Except this time it did work. I finally understood. *La raya* meant stingray.

It explained the shooting flames of agony. I knew exactly what had to be done from watching *Friends*, the one where Joey says pee will cure Monica's jellyfish sting, but he can't do it so Chandler does. I didn't like the idea. I've never been turned on by the thought of a golden shower. In fact it's disgusting, but at that moment all I wanted was for those two cute Tico boys to pee on me. "O.K., O.K. I get it. It's a stingray, so do what you have to do. Pee on me, please, now hurry. Just do it. Pee on my foot! Pee on me!" I shrieked between blasts of pain. They both stopped dead and looked at me with blank expressions.

"What are you waiting for? I'm dying over here." All I could think of was the Crocodile Hunter man and how he got hit by a stingray right in his chest, and it killed him. I didn't want to go the same way. "God damn it, pee on my foot to neutralize the venom." What was wrong with them? Everyone knew this, even Joey.

Alejandro was the first to figure out what I was saying. He looked at Marco and explained in Spanish what I was demanding of them. They turned in unison, with visible expressions of disgust and amusement, and looked down at me writhing in the sand.

Alejandro said, "It's *la raya*, the only way to stop the pain is to submerge the foot in boiling hot water for two hours."

Then Marco kindly offered to fulfill my request of peeing on me if it would stop the screaming.

So where do you find boiling hot water on a deserted beach, miles from the lovely little tourist town with its restaurants, yoga studios, coffee shops and medical clinic? Why, of course, at the fisherman's dilapidated hut hidden in the trees. They carried me through the brush, leaving a thick trail of blood streaming out of my foot and onto the sand. I was left rolling on the porch as they roused the fisherman and explained the problem. I have no idea how he managed to produce a big bucket full of boiling water so fast from the back of a 200-square-foot shack, but there it was, bubbling and steaming. It took all three of them to hold me down as they plunged my foot into the boiling water. I admit it immediately took some of the stinging pain away, as the only sensation I had was the burning of my flesh from the knee down. Maybe I wouldn't die from the stingray sting, but death from the gangrene in my burned off stump of a leg was still a distinct possibility.

As I sat on the porch, foot jammed in a white bucket of scalding water, the three men told me stories. The old man had been stung six times on the same rocks where the ray got me. He pulled up his pant leg revealing the large scars all over his feet that he proudly displayed like Rich-ard Dreyfuss in *Jaws*. My cut was barely a centimeter long across the top of my toe but after looking at him, I knew it would be with me forever. Both Alejandro and Marco had grown up surfing those same waters and had never been stung. They emphatically stated it was good luck to be chosen by *la raya*, but I figured that's like saying getting shit on by a bird is good luck, so the target doesn't feel like a loser, even though he's covered in bird shit.

As the nerves in my toes began to activate once again, I felt a new, sticky sensation. I looked down into the bucket and was greeted by a view of chunky tomato stew. The blood had turned the water a Campbell's tomato soup red, and it was starting to coagulate into one solid mass. The fisherman took the bucket of congealed Beth blood and disappeared into the back room. I have no idea what he did with that mess but we repeated this routine three or four times. The pain was constant, the source alternating between the venomous sting and the poaching. And then, just as if a switch went off, the pain subsided. I looked at my watch. Two hours had passed, exactly as Alejandro said it would. Whew! Time to get back to civilization.

The boys wrapped my foot tightly in a towel. I had to use the ladies' room—or more accurately, the hole in the floor—so I made my way to the back of the shack. As I stepped down the towel fell off my foot and blood began shooting out of my toe and up the wall! It was a scene worthy of Tarantino, and all I could think about was Mr. Blonde chopping off Marvin's ear in *Reservoir Dogs*, except this was my very real toe. I yelled out in horror, and the boys came running. They all stopped dead and stared at my foot. Who knew the heart could pump hard enough to shoot blood that high in the air through one small toe? The fisherman made the first move, grabbed the towel and wrapped my foot as the two boys snapped out of it, picked me up, and carried me to the truck.

The beautiful beach drive was far less romantic in this direction, and it seemed to go on forever. I held the towel tightly to my foot, but the blood just kept pumping, turning the terrycloth pink, then scarlet. I tossed the towel out the window and grabbed another. Two towels later we made it into Nosara and pulled up at the clinic. The doctor was busy so we waited in the tiny immaculate lobby and I continued to bleed all over the floor. A little Consuela-ish cleaning lady, complete with yellow rubber gloves (just like on *Family Guy*), tottered by every ten minutes or so to smile and say "no, no" as she mopped up after me.

By the time I got in to see the doctor, I had been bleeding for well over four hours. As he stitched up my still oozing toe, he kindly informed me of the proper procedure for neutralizing the ray's sting. He said heat was good for deactivating the proteins in the poison; however, simmering over a low heat was just as effective as a rapid boil and much more comfortable for still-living flesh. Two stitches later the bleeding finally stopped. I had my foot nicely bandaged and was returned to my surfer dude saviors, Marco and Alejandro. I wondered, should I tell them about the slow-cooker method for the benefit of the next victim? I decided against it. Why rob someone else of the adventure?

As the boys dropped me off, I could tell they were glad to be rid of me and my constantly erupting toe. I hoped they managed to get the crusty blood off the dashboard of their spotless truck. That wouldn't be good for business.

Now, eight hours later, I am face down, buck-naked on the bathroom tiles in my best slasher-flick pose. Blood covers the floor and there are red handprints on the walls and the sink. It's no use trying to drag myself off the floor. I lie in the pool of blood for an eternity. My hair is matted and my body is covered in a skin-tight bodysuit of blood. But why am I naked, smashing my face into the floor? Could I really have lost that much blood from a tiny stingray bite on my toe? I guess I bled for about five hours. I must have gotten up in the night to use the bathroom, stood up too fast and then passed out face first on the floor. That's it. No robbers, no gunmen, no monster wave, no crazed psychopath, not even a giant shark. My broken nose, black eyes, swollen lips, and huge foot are the result of one little stingray, a bucket of boiling water, and an old fisherman in a tiny hut on a deserted beach.

Two weeks later, as I board the flight home, I glance down through bruised eyes at the stingray victim—my burnt right toe. I have dubbed him Freddy (as in Freddy Krueger) due to their striking resemblance. A drop of blood oozes from beneath the bandage. What? Still? I never should have named my toe Freddy Krueger—Freddy is coming home and Freddy doesn't like me.

★

Beth Mercer is a writer and script supervisor based in Vancouver, BC. She has worked in film and television for 25 years on series such as The X-Files, Battlestar Galactica, Smallville, Alcatraz, Dead Zone, *and many more. Beth teaches a course in Script Supervision. When not keeping track of the famous and infamous on a film set, Beth can be found exploring the globe, skiing off cornices, biking down volcanoes, and surfing the little waves. She inherited her passion for travel, mountains, and writing from her mother. Beth's website: www.travelswithmyselfandanother.com*

DANA TALUSANI

A Real Good Deal

Banana hammocks and twinkly tits in Cancún.

"I HAVE SUCH GOOD NEWS FOR YOU, NANA," MY MOTHER-IN-law says to my husband. I imagine her Indian accent lilting in excitement over the phone line. "That surprise trip you were thinking for Dana? For birthday? Well, I did some checking around on my break, just looking, and I found incredible deal. Amazing place, price so low! And best news—price even better if book by the end of today!"

"Well, that's great, Mom," my husband says hesitantly. "You're sure about this place? It's not too much trouble?"

"No trouble," she insists. "You busy with work. Leave things to me. Everything great."

"You really think we can afford this?" I ask my husband, buckling myself into the airline seat. "I mean, it's sweet and all…"

"Mom totally took care of it," he says breezily. "She scored us a crazy package rate. When she called with the price, I almost couldn't believe it."

"Your mom is downright spooky. She can sniff out the cheapest deals on anything," I say.

"She's Indian," my spouse smirks. "It's in her blood. Tell an American person they're cheap and they'll be offended. Tell an Indian? They'll smile proudly and say, 'Thank you very much.'"

"Welcome to Cancún!" says the greeter at the resort. "Complimentary Tequila Sunrise for you?" He hands us cups of a boozy, coral-tinged concoction.

"Free booze on arrival?" I whisper to my husband. "I like this place already."

"Your room is on the third floor," the attendant says, handing us an envelope. "There are keys and a resort map and some informational things on activities in here."

We get to the door, and my husband opens the envelope. He chuckles. "O.K…they gave us six room keys. For the two of us. How many keys do they expect us to lose in three days?"

"I don't know," I say, looking around the room, "but maybe *that* has something to do with it." I point to the wall above the wet bar.

"Holy crap!" My husband spots the six mounted bottles of liquor—with spigot dispensers—hanging upside down on the wall. "It's like a booze soda fountain." He grabs a shot glass and heads for the tequila.

"Whoa, Pancho Villa," I warn. "Stop right there. Is this stuff included, or is it extra?"

My husband squirts himself a tequila, sucks it down and winks. "All-inclusive, baby."

I shake my head. "You're unbelievable."

The raucous sounds of a Mariachi band boom from the downstairs lobby. "Wanna unpack first or just head down and wander around?" he asks.

"Let's unpack a little first." Then I do what I always do when I first get to a hotel: turn on the television.

Up pops a pair of balloon-sized breasts, bouncing up and down with vigor. "Give it to me, baby," she moans, grinding her pelvis into the man underneath her.

"Whoa! Porn! Honey, get a load of this. What kind of perv had this room before us? I am going to be so pissed off if this comes up on our hotel bill. Inclusive, my ass. I'm sure they charge you for porn."

"Babe, relax. I'm sure it's fine."

"No, really. Go check the information booklet. No way am I paying for this." I flick the channel on the remote. I'm greeted with the sight of a perky, oiled male ass. "Ack!" I fumble around the room for a hotel television guide.

"Nope," my husband calls from the sitting area. "Porn is free!"

"Good thing," I call back, scanning the television listings, "because we have five channels of it."

"Hand me the sunscreen, would you?" I ask, arranging towels on a chaise lounge. "You have to admit, this is a beautiful pool."

"Yeah, but it's deserted," my husband says, handing me the Coppertone. "It's eleven o'clock."

"You heard how late that party went last night. I'm sure people are sleeping it off. It'll crowd up soon."

My husband browses the activities board posted by the towel station. "Tequila blackjack at 11:30."

"Ugh, Jesus! We just ate breakfast! How do people do this?"

"It's vacation, baby," my man smiles. "Some people go big or go home."

Some people do show up for tequila blackjack: a pack of young, ruddy-faced men with Canadian accents. They arrive with beers in their hands, gambling chips in their pockets, and sunburns. My husband can't resist. I wave him on and return to my book.

Within half an hour, things get animated and loud at the blackjack table. The Canadians are already several beers in and hurling good-natured insults at one another. I wander over to investigate.

"Saskatchewan!" my husband announces, beer in hand. "It's ten degrees below zero there right now! This is Brian, Kevin, Kurt, and Devin. They work on fishing boats. They come here every year!"

The boys nod.

"The fucking winter, eh, goddamn cold and long," Devin says.

"We save up and spend two weeks here every year," Brian says. "Can't beat the prices."

"Or action," adds Kurt.

"Or the view," Kevin wags his eyebrows at his buddies. They all chortle.

I glance at the pool area. "The view?"

They break into fits of laughter. "Wait until afternoon," Devin leers. "You'll see."

By 2:00 P.M. the Saskatchewan lads are well into their cups.

"Damn, those boys must have had one cold, hard winter," I say to my hubby. "How do their livers survive the two-week stay here?"

"Stamina of the young and the unlaid," he says. "Hey, do you want to grab some lun—oh my, what is that?"

"What?"

He jerks his head hard left, eyes wide.

I look at the buxom, bottle-blonde in an impossibly small bikini. Well, the bottom half of a bikini, anyways. "Those tits are too good to be true," I say.

"But they…sparkle," he says.

Indeed, they do sparkle, because the woman has embellished her titties with dangly, gold chandelier-type nipple rings, encrusted with little gemstones that wink and gleam in the midday sun. They bob and entrance us. Neither of us can look away.

"We gotta look away," I say, grabbing my book. "We're staring like magpies."

"But they're mesmerizing," he laughs.

Her companion, a male, is nearly as sparkly and so tanned that he's the color of tree bark. He boasts two heavy gold bracelets, a diamond-encrusted watch, and a medallion around his neck. He compensates for such heavy-handedness by being nearly naked from the waist down.

"What do you call those things?" I hiss to my husband.

"Banana hammocks, babe," he snickers. The man turns around to adjust his chaise lounge and I'm treated to a full view of his backside.

"Jesus," I say, "you know what this means, don't you?"

"What?"

"Eurotrash."

Eurotrash. By four in the afternoon, the pool area is teeming and pulsating with oiled bodies, fancy body piercings, bleached and coiffed hair, and audacious jewelry. They're everywhere, they're heavily liquored up, and they're incredibly friendly. They buzz from lounge chair to lounge chair like a welcome wagon on steroids.

"Hello, there, darling! Who might you be?"

"Haven't seen you around. Did you just get in? Isn't it fabulous?"

"Don't tell me. Americans, right? I just love Americans…"

We've been asked out for predinner cocktails by Roxy and Daniel. Roger and Gigi ask if we'd like to join them for dinner. Stephan and Bianca want to know if we're interested in sharing a taxi to a chic discotheque later in the evening. All of the attention is beginning to make me grumpy. "*Gaaa*, can't people leave us alone?" I mumble into my margarita. "Can't they tell we're on a romantic getaway?"

"They're just having a good time, blowing off some steam," my husband shrugs. "Nothing wrong with being sociable and meeting new people. It's kind of a party crowd."

"No shit," I say, surveying the pool area for the Canadians. They're bobbing up and down in the hot tub, red-faced and sweaty, half-draped around some very young, bronzed babes.

"So I guess that's a 'no' to dinner with Gigi and Rog?" he chuckles.

"I'm interested in having dinner with you," I say. "Just you."

"And maybe watch a little quality television after? Eh? Whaddaya say, baby?"

"Shut up." I give him a swat with my book. "Perv."

It isn't until late afternoon, on our second full day of vacation, when we encounter a man at the pool bar smoking a Havana cigar, wearing a large, neon Hawaiian shirt and *nothing* on the bottom half of his person, that we realize what kind of situation we've stumbled into.

Nobody even blinks an eye at no-pants man. He hangs around, has a few more drinks and chats amiably with the bartender.

"How can that be O.K.?" I hiss at my bug-eyed husband.

"I seriously don't know," he says. "They just must have different kinds of…rules or something here."

"More like NO rules," I shoot back. "Is that even sanitary?! Walking around just…flopping like that?"

"Well, look at all those ladies at the pool," he says. "They aren't exactly wearing much either…"

BOOM.

And then it hits us: multiple room keys, five channels of free porn, unlimited liquor, Eurotrash, unabashed nudity, plus strange couples who are eager to get to know us better.

"Oh my God," I gasp, looking at my husband in shock. "Fuckity-fuck! Your mother! Your cheap-ass mother booked us at a swinger's resort!"

My husband is laughing so hard he can hardly speak. "Babe! She didn't know! She no way knew about this."

"There's a guy walking around here with no pants, for chrissakes!"

My husband snorts and wipes away a tear. "What are you really mad about, Honeytits? That my mother booked us at a swinger's resort? Or that we're so stupid that it took us two whole days to figure it out?"

"Yeah, yeah, Mr. Funnypants. You keep laughing, but need I remind you: we have one more full day left here."

So how *do* you spend your last full day of vacation at a swinger's resort? My husband and I decided to completely go with it. What else were we gonna do? We played tequila blackjack. We challenged the Canadians to a rousing game of beach volleyball. We screamed out answers during poolside "Who Wants to be a Millionaire?" trivia. We kicked ass at Dirty Word Bingo. The last half-hour at the pool, before we had to pack for the trip home, I took off my bikini top, cheerful and defiant.

"How do I look?" I asked my husband.

He lifted his margarita glass in a toast. "Best damn piece of Eurotrash I've ever seen."

To this day, my mother-in-law still likes to recall her instrumental role in snagging us the vacation deal of the century.

"Remember that time I got you that real good deal?" she will say smugly. "Crazy good deal for place like that. Super nice place, right? Amazing place."

My husband and I will share a smile. "Yep, you really caught us a good one there," my husband will say.

"Amazing," I agree.

"Heh," she will say, quite satisfied with herself. "Who know? Maybe, after I retire this job? I know what I do—I become travel agent."

Dana Talusani lives in the Rocky Mountains and is a humor, parenting, lifestyle and food writer. She is the author of the snarky and eclectic blog The Kitchen Witch *(www.thekitchwitch.com). Her work has been featured on* CNN.com, Today.com, The Hufffington Post, Scary Mommy, Purple Clover, *and In* the Powder Room, *among others. She is currently at work on her first novel.*

The Battle of Waterkloof

Bruce Lee vs. the Namibian Baboon Army.

NAMIBIA WAS FOUNDED ON TWO INDISPUTABLE TRUTHS. ONE: it never rains. Thus I lose my favorite excuse to opt out of a hike. Two: every Asian person is Bruce Lee. These two random facts play pivotally in the attack of the baboons.

The Waterkloof Trail, which exists only in a theoretical sense, consists of 17 kilometers of yellow markers. My friend Bearcat and I are told to follow them religiously.

"Oh, and take this map too," says one of the park rangers. On a crumpled piece of paper he sketches a crooked circle and scribbles small words along the perimeter. This is a Picasso of maps and a leap of faith to follow.

Our hike begins on a high note. We talk, we laugh, and we trap tadpoles in our baseball caps. With Taylor Swift blasting on my iPod, I am having the time of my life. "You smell that?" I ask, navigating through a thicket of tall grass.

"Smells like piss."

"*Really* strong piss."

"It's getting worse."

When I can find nothing comical to say about this pungency, a sense of urgency ensues. We inspect our shoes for rhinoceros diarrhea and find none. Then we scan for lurking predators, recalling from a recent game drive that it is a male lion's territorial nature to urinate on everything. No lions. Good.

Then we identify the source—a rotting zebra. I dart away from the carcass before my breakfast returns as projectile vomit. My previous craving for zebra steak has evaporated, but Bearcat has already removed his pocketknife. "What cut would you like for lunch?"

We continue and the midpoint marker materializes after a protracted climb. We feast on Goldfish, apples, tangerines, and beef jerky while mesmerized by the landscape beneath. This place has a natural sense of order to it.

"You think they have wi-fi up here?" I ask.

"Probably not."

"O.K."

Only three hours in and a record-breaking finish looms. Encouraged, fed and rested, we begin our descent, fearless and unsuspecting. But much to our irritation, the yellow markers, aplenty thus far, have developed a newfound penchant for hiding. I haven't had to look for anything so hard since *Where's Waldo? In Hollywood*. Also, good vision, I discover, doesn't come easier with age. Neither does patience. With our confidence sky high and patience wearing thin, we invent our own shortcut. It takes us around a hill through human-sized thorn bushes and then down a waterfall on algae-slick rocks. We blaze through every improbable opening, driven by the intangible concept of "manhood" and the unthinkable concept of turning back. When we stumble into a dreamlike cove borrowed from the movie *Avatar*, it finally hits us— we are lost. Recognizing the severity of our stupidity, we backtrack desperately up the hill. Forty minutes later, the sacred yellow marker reappears.

"I never once doubted our abilities," I announce.

Bearcat takes a celebratory dip in the river, very much bearlike. I can't tell if he is trying to cool off or catch salmon. But his victory lap proves premature. The river leads us to a valley tucked between two towering cliffs—the proud home of hundreds of baboons. When their piercing war cries descend upon us, our immediate reaction is denial.

"It can't be because of us," I plead to the air. "We just got here. Besides, we humans are distant relatives, honored guests who have traveled from afar to visit."

But with each measured step we take, the cacophony explodes tenfold. There is no turning back now, not without backtracking thirteen kilometers and getting lost again. Alternatively, if we can somehow explain our situation to these estranged cousins—perhaps mention an ailing grandfather—will they commiserate and let us through? But how do we do this? With our eyes?

"Don't look them in the eye," warns Bearcat. He removes his baseball cap to wipe his forehead.

If I were the volatile drama queen in our partnership, Bearcat would be the cool-headed ranger in good times and bad. Now though, his expression betrays raw fear. Make no mistake—death is a distinct possibility here, if not from direct attack, then certainly from subsequent infection. (Fun fact: Untreated rabies can lead to coma and death.) I take his expression as a cue to pick up something sharp and put an angry rap song on my iPod. Where is the face paint when you need it? Being called "Bruce Lee" by everyone in Africa used to annoy me; now it offers a possible escape. Would my Asian heritage demand the same respect from King Baboon?

I am mortally scared of combat. Shaken though I am, I can smell a character-defining opportunity. Will this be the grand stage where my untried white-belt karate moves wow the world? Or, at the other extreme, a zoological experiment to see if I can outrun a baboon? Bearcat and I exchange a knowing nod and take the brave first step. I resist the urge to peek behind my shoulder for fear of coming across as weak. As the baboons' bellows of rage reach a crescendo, the past reading I've done on survival springs to mind.

Jungle survival, especially on the subject of predatory encounter, has long been a hot topic. Countless literature and academic research, which likely includes several Ph.D. theses, have offered differing views on what to do and what not to do. Yours truly happens to have a massive appetite for such information.

Peter Allison, author of two candid African safari guides, said it all in his book title, *Whatever You Do, Don't Run*. According to wildlife experts, animals often mock charge to see if you flinch. The best thing to do in these situations, they all claim, is to simply stand tall. "Food runs," Allison's friend Alpheus cunningly puts it, "and there is nothing in [the wild] you can outrun anyway." Inaction was Allison's recipe to surviving a standoff against two male lions. When I was reading his encounter from the safety of my couch, it made a world of sense to me. "Just. Stand. There." I'd repeated to myself, sipping warm Ovaltine. *I mean, shit, how hard can that be?*

Fast-forward two months and here I am in Naukluft, presented with the opportunity of a lifetime to prove just that. For all the discipline with which I committed Allison's words to memory, it takes one swift glance at a baboon's fearsome teeth to swing my pendulum of indecision. In *A Walk in the Woods*, Bill Bryson offered a more cynical approach. "If you are in an open space with no weapons and a grizzly comes for you," Bryson wrote, "run. You may as well," he added, "if nothing else, it will give you something to do with the last seven seconds of your life."

To run, or not to run, that is the question. Do I bet on expertise derived from years of field experience, or side with my vulnerable literary idol? In the end, I choose the latter—the coward in me relates to Bryson's human shortcomings. Besides, being the elder of the two, Bryson has a longer track record of survival. In times like this, trust the numbers.

The baboons jump and wail and flail their arms. Then finally, the army charges our way. I freeze on the spot, moving only my arm to reach for Bearcat. "It has been an honor" is what I would have said had I not been so busy crapping my pants.

Then, a miracle.

They halt ten feet short of our defense line. They hover back and forth behind an invisible fence. I can see aggression draining from their faces. Then slowly and reluctantly, they move on. Perhaps they sensed my readiness to fight them to the bitter end. Or perhaps they knew better than to fuck with the Bruce Lee.

The moment Bearcat and I reach the other end of the valley, we toss our weapons and sprint up the hill to safety. Just like that, a showdown between primates is averted. And just like that, these baboons live to see another day.

★

Gerald Yeung is the author of Wannabe Backpackers: The Latin American and Kenyan Journey of Five Spoiled Teenagers. *His futile pursuit of the American Dream was documented on the Hong Kong government youth blog. Now living in San Jose, California, outside baboon domain, he spends his free time running away from dogs.*

NIGEL ROTH

Cold London Summer

A tale of how sex changes everything.

STEPHANIE WAS 26 WHEN I MET HER IN LONDON. SHE WAS taller than any other girl I had dated and more attractive and more confident. She walked like a model because she was, and she conversed like an actress because she was that also. This was far too good to be true, but I didn't really want to believe my own wisdom.

That first night we drank at a bar in Islington. Islington was the new West End (whatever that meant), and the bar was billed as trendy and "kicking." Stephanie's smile was not the first thing I noticed about her when she swaggered in. She wore a tight Lycra top. Her breasts had a perfect shape to them—not too full, with a slight bottom-heaviness that accentuated her nipples.

She sat and we said hello. She said I was handsome. I laughed and said she was beautiful. She was beautiful. In truth though, I was horny and she was stunning. We met in the middle out of politeness.

I ordered whiskey; she ordered Scotch. I drank slowly; she gulped greedily. I ran my fingers through my hair;

she swung her head and blond-amber curls unfurled and regrouped. I missed a breath; she just smiled. I talked about India; she spoke of friends. I described my dreams; she listened, teared up, let her head fall to the left. I noticed men staring at her; she never took her eyes off of me. I was, I believe, in shock. She was just beginning to relax.

When I told her of my careless marriage, Stephanie stretched out her hand to hold mine. I had given her the cue, fed her the line. She had seized it. I looked at her hand; eye-to-eye would be too soon. She squeezed; I smiled.

"Another drink?" I asked.

"At my place," Stephanie suggested.

The play was complete. The curtain fell as we walked to her shiny car, and I heard the audience roar as we drove north along St John Street.

Her small flat had complexities I could not have imagined. The kitchen was tiny and brand new. The table pulled out from a sidewall and a leg sprung menacingly out to support it. The cold tap was on the wrong side and the socket was underneath the table. The kettle was in the corner cupboard that could only open if the washing machine was pulled out first.

"They put it together so cheaply," Stephanie explained, as she made coffee for us.

The milk, sugar and coffee—which were in long, round sachets with Café Noir written on the side—went in the cup first. Stephanie mixed them together and then poured in the water. The whole thing fizzed and foamed, and we took it to the living room.

"It's only a small place," Stephanie said, "but it's mine." I agreed, then quickly added that it was good to have your own place.

We sat on good furniture with strange patterns. We drank the foamy coffee with our knees together. Stephanie began to tell me about her acting career. I listened, intent on keeping my stare at eye level. I became aroused just listening to her. When she spoke, her mouth would stay open after she released the last word. Just a few seconds enough for my imagination.

"I started young," she said. "They say that's a good way to get into acting, right? Start young?"

"I've heard that," I said, hoping to sound sincere. I was sincere, just distracted.

"My first role." Stephanie pointed to a picture in her album. She'd brought it down while I was trying to turn around in the bathroom without having to back out. She was 12 in the photo. She looked older to me. She was playing Sinbad. Her pirate's bandana and high boots looked authentic. She made a good boy.

We sat together and looked through the album, from cover to cover. After the pirate, Stephanie appeared in a play about drug abuse called *Getting the Needle*. She was "twenty-two" she said "and a few months." She smiled as she anticipated my question.

"I took a break from school and college, you know," she laughed, and kissed me. I kissed her too. Her lips were strong and full, she pressed hard. Her tongue was clumsy.

After, she said, "Well, that didn't take long, did it? You're a cheeky one!" I smiled at the thought. It hadn't taken very long at all. A few hours. My actress.

"Do you want to see more modeling stuff?" I did, but I also wanted to make love to her.

"Sure, show me," I said.

That called for more coffee and a cigarette for Stephanie.

"They're only mild. I don't smoke much. Just...you know." I truly didn't but I nodded.

She held her cigarette like my grandfather used to, between her thumb and first finger, and she turned it to face her after each drag. What a mix this girl was. She drank Scotch and held her cigarettes like a gangster, and yet she acted and modeled professionally. And, she made frothy coffee, which I sipped as she showed me page after page of lingerie and swimsuit magazine tear-outs.

"No more photos," she said, as she closed the book.

"They were great."

"You just wanted to see me with my kit off, didn't you?" Of course I did, who wouldn't?

"No, of course not, but you are beautiful."

"You think so?" Stephanie said, dragging the last from the Embassy No 1.

"Yes," I said, almost laughing. She was incredibly beautiful. And she kissed me again.

"Do you want to have breakfast with me?" she asked.

The sun caught the mirror and made me look pale. But I couldn't help smiling. "My actress," I said softly and laughed at my good fortune.

"Coffee here," Stephanie called from the tiny kitchen. *Sexy voice*, I thought. *A little guttural.*

We sat by her window and looked out at Temple Fortune high street on a Saturday morning. For a moment I pretended I was alone. Not just alone, but lonely. A straggler. With no day ahead of me. A whole Saturday. I savored the despair, knowing I was alive.

Stephanie sipped her coffee. She slurped the froth and licked her lips. Her hair was beautifully messy, my actress in the morning.

"I've got something to tell you," she said, without warning. No facial expression, just a confessional tilt of her head.

"What is it?" I put my empty coffee mug to my lips to diffuse the appearance of caring too much about what she might tell me. Already I cared too much.

"It's not too bad. I just need to tell you." I resisted wondering. I focused hard, gave a look of concern, rather than worry. Not worry, fear. *Don't take away my actress*, I thought.

"When I was young, I used a lot of drugs," she said, pronouncing drugs, "da-rugs" as if sounded out for a child. I nodded, feeling slightly nauseous and lightheaded. "I'm clean now. But it was a bad time. A few bad years, you know what I mean?"

I searched. Why did no answer seem right? My silence had been too long.

"Do you still like me?"

Of course I liked her. God, I almost loved her. Loved her?

"Shit happens," I said. I had never taken a drug in my life. Unless you include aspirin. "As long as you're clean now, that's what counts. You are here and you are you."

"Well, it took a while to get here. I was out of it for about five years. Well, a bit longer really. On the streets for a lot of the time."

She seemed quite blasé about it, so I imitated tone. "Made you who you are." Stupid comment.

"Yep, that's for sure," Stephanie said, and we finished our frothy coffee holding hands and watching the sun bleach the Saturday shoppers.

That night we made love. It started in the kitchen at my hotel room in Knightsbridge. Kissing and holding each other's hair, then laughing and pulling our t-shirts off. Revealing my actress: her slim, smooth body, her long legs, her dolphin tattoo, her exquisite breasts, her firm nipples. I took every part of her in my mouth and savored her sweetness. I used my tongue to explore her and she caressed me firmly with strong hands. At some point, a point I can never guess at or preempt, she guided me into her and breathed in sharply as I entered. She bucked once against me, began to moan in that same moment and ran her nails up my back, and I felt the skin tear from me, and she came, screaming; long, deep, guttural screams, and closed her eyes, and smiled, and held me tight.

It was only later I realized I had not reached orgasm. She had, in a matter of minutes. So quickly that I had felt slow and somehow less excited. I was excited and yet I had been fine to let it go. I felt strong, masculine, and proud, like a quiet hero. I was my own audience, and I felt I played my part well.

Our sex was always like that, fast and strong. Almost manly. I thought I would raise the subject over whiskey in the pub that evening. But, sensing my question, or at least my curiosity, Stephanie preempted me.

"I need to tell you something else about me. Something I'm not proud of, but it happened, and like you said, it made me." I braced myself, that numb, nauseated feeling returning.

"I don't know how to say this," she mumbled. "Well, it's not that bad, I suppose."

Tell me now, I thought, but I nodded nonchalantly.

"I had sex with another girl for this politician. You know, just fumbling around in front of him. He never joined in." She sipped her Scotch.

I smiled, I think out of nervousness or out of shock, or out of anger. All three maybe. "That's it?" I asked, faking surprise at how insignificant it seemed. It worked.

"Well, I did it a few times. You know, for a few months. Couple of times a week. We were just pretending really, but he liked it."

"Pretending?"

"Yeah, you know, bit of kissing, licking, fingering. Nothing really." She downed her Scotch in one gulp. "He paid for my car and the flat, silly sod. I'll never do it again. You know. It was a one off."

A one off, I repeated in my head. This girl was a one off. The feeling of nausea had not passed. I couldn't finish my whiskey. I thought of walking out, leaving, going north to The Lake District, clearing my head. But then again, it was fairly harmless, wasn't it? And a car and a flat isn't a bad reward. What would I do to get those things if I had to? Who was I to judge?

"Well," Stephanie asked. She had been talking to me. I had been so deep in my emotional spiral, I hadn't heard her. "Want to play some pool or not?"

"Sure, yes, why not?" I managed. I ordered more whiskey and played pool with my actress.

I returned from New York the following Saturday morning and had dinner at Stephanie's that evening. It was good to see her, tall and beautiful and barefoot, her nipples showing through her cotton tank top. We made love in the bath, and we lay on the bed with a cool breeze blowing against our nakedness.

"Do you like New York?" Stephanie asked.

"Yes, I do. It suits me very well."

"Would you live there?" She had read my mind.

"I would. I dream more when I'm there."

"I missed you."

I held her. She had become softer since I last felt her body, smoother.

"I know you're going to think I'm crazy," she said, "but there's something I need to ask you." *Ask me* sounded less threatening than *tell me*. Or was I just becoming desensitized to Stephanie's heart-wrenching secrets?

"Tell me anything," I said boldly, hoping Stephanie would tell me nothing at all.

"Well," she started in that odd kindergarten voice again, "before I met you, I was with someone, someone who's a girl." She paused for my reply.

"A girl," I said genuinely relieved.

"Bridget," she said.

"Bridget."

"Yes. I was with her for three years."

"O.K.," I said, "that's fine."

"You don't mind?"

"No. Why should I?"

"Well," she began, with the kid voice, "I'm still seeing her."

"You're still seeing her?"

"Yeah. Only now and again."

"But you're seeing me."

"Yeah. But it's different with Bridget. Not better," she added quickly, "just different, you know."

I think I sighed audibly.

"Are you O.K. with that?" Stephanie asked, her voice trembling slightly. What could I say? I preached openness. I celebrated sexual diversity. I argued with everyone for experimentation and empirical evolution.

"Of course I'm O.K.," I said, and I was.

"Really?"

"Absolutely," I said.

"Good, because I want you to meet her."

It struck me for the first time in our short but loving three-month affair, that I might be the victim of subtle manipulation. But why? To what possible end? I was dating a model and actress, a beautiful woman who came every time I fucked her and who wanted me to meet her female lover. Where was the downside?

"She's on her way. She'll be here in a few minutes. You're going to love her."

I couldn't think of a downside.

Bridget was as beautiful and as amber-blond as Stephanie. She was shorter, and had a fuller figure. More womanly, less androgynous. Stephanie said Bridget's ass was gorgeous, and Bridget bent over and proved it. Bridget said she loved Stephanie's neck and kissed and held it as we drank Scotch. Stephanie told me how Bridget could spend hours between her legs, and she spread herself as if to invite a demonstration.

This was pure sex. In its purest form. Lust. A raw, desperate longing that I immediately envied. I watched as they found reasons to touch each other, pinch each other, and caress each other. I was losing my actress, if, that is, I ever had her. As I watched Bridget and Stephanie kiss, I knew I never did.

When I came back to the living room with a glass of water, they were gone. I listened for their voices and could hear them in the bedroom. Breathless whispers, moans, and hard smacking lips. I imagined two boats in a harbor crashing together with the tide. I heard them moaning and stretching and I heard light pats against their skin, and yelps as they enjoyed each other.

I put my water down and took my jacket from the closet. I tied my laces and left the glass in Stephanie's tiny kitchen. I turned and walked to the door. I was leaving the warmth of the flat for the cold evening air. Leaving the candlelight for the dark night. I listened for a moment longer to the women kissing and moaning and whispering their love.

"I love you so much," Stephanie was panting, "do you still love me?"

I smiled at her insecurity. This stunning woman. This model. This tall, slender goddess.

"Of course I do," Bridget answered in her sweet melodic voice, "as much now as when you were a fella."

I stood. Very still. The door ajar. The cold air rushing in, keeping me from blacking out as the blood rushed from my head. My heart thumped. My eyes were staring but seeing nothing. I thought: my actress. I closed the door behind me and stepped into the honesty of a cold London summer.

Nigel Roth was born in London, England, and grew up wherever his family found work. His father was a journeyman dreamer, and his mother managed the office at an old-age home. He moved to Canada when he was two years old, while his father headed north to the oil rigs above the Brooks Range, until the family moved back to England and to a series of homes across the country. Nigel attended London Guildhall University and Birkbeck College in London.

VANESSA VAN DOREN

Going Feral
in Filoha

*The stool collector: a monkey-business researcher has to
hand over her own business.*

"ARE YOU SICK? WERE YOU HAVING DIARRHEA?!" MAT
yelled as I came slinking back from the camp's toilet.

Fuuuuck. "Err…what?" I mumbled. Apparently my plan
to unobtrusively drift over to the toilet for the twelfth
time that day on the pretense of "admiring the view"
wasn't all that subtle.

"Tell me your symptoms and I'll look them up!" Mat
said, opening our worn copy of *Where There is No Doctor*
and rifling through the chapters with his long fingers.

Some people ask for their coworker's opinion on the
latest *Game of Thrones* episode and others ask about her
exploding bowel situation. While listening to Office
Manager Kenneth salivate over his favorite King's Landing brothel scene does get uncomfortable, my day-to-day
workplace mortification hit a fiery new zenith while I was
in Ethiopia for fieldwork.

I had been living in a one-man tent in a remote outpost of Awash National Park for the past month, collecting

genetic samples (read: monkey poop) from the hamadryas baboons I was studying. And it had become recently clear that there was something terribly wrong with my GI tract.

At first things went great. I'd been rising before the sun with the project manager, Mat, and research assistant, Teklu, walking out to the baboons' sleeping cliff, and following them from sunup to when they settled in for sleep at a new cliff. It was wonderful to begin each day like that: hearing the baboons grunting and murmuring as they awoke; arriving at the top of the cliff just as the sun began to peek over the horizon; watching it slowly warm and color the land below. I was walking up to 20 kilometers a day in searing heat and navigating acacia thorns that ripped at my skin and clothes. I finished each day by rejuvenating my dirty, sweaty, exhausted self in the hot springs. I was sunburnt, never quite clean, and covered in festering mosquito bites. And I felt great—I felt invincible. I was impressed with how adaptable and resilient my body was proving to be.

But at some point, I got overconfident. I had decided to toughen my body up (inside and out) by doing everything the Ethiopians did, including eating anything put in front of me. Sometimes I wasn't even sure what I'd eaten until after it was already down the hatch, like the time Mat invited me to try "the best part of the goat."

"What do you think?" he'd said, mirth bubbling just below the surface of his sharp blue eyes.

"Kind of chewy, I guess. What is this?" I'd replied, tentatively poking the tough, fibrous white meat with my tongue.

"Goat testicle! Oh, the kids love it here. It's really the best part of the whole animal." Unable to contain himself any longer, his face split into a wide, white-toothed grin.

I'm still not completely sure what particular culinary delight led to my poo predicament. It could have been the *firfir* I picked at throughout one long, hot day following the baboons across the scrub desert. The mashed up stale bread and leftover tomato paste festered in a sweating Tupperware, a sure sign that we needed to replenish our food stores at the village market. It could have been the *tibs* I ate during our trip to the Metahara marketplace that weekend—spicy sautéed goat meat, onions, and green peppers on a bed of *injera*. You eat this dish with your hands, ripping off a piece of the pancake-like *injera* bread and wrapping it around a mouthful of meat and veggies. Maybe it was the unfiltered water and *tella* (homemade beer) I'd drunk while visiting our cook's parents' home, or the neon-orange *tej* (honey wine) I'd sipped out of a round-bottomed *berele*.

In any case, my guts started feeling pretty weird one evening as I crawled into my tent. With characteristic overzealousness, I had brought 15 seminal primatology books to facilitate complete immersion in my work, only to find after book number three that reading about apes and monkeys after spending a 12-hour day engrossed in baboon social life gets to be a *bit* much. Nonetheless, I picked up my current book, *Gorillas in the Mist*, by Dian Fossey, and delved back into her life with the mountain gorillas in Rwanda. My headlamp began to flicker as the batteries expired, so I switched it off and rolled over to sleep.

I awoke an hour later, drenched in sweat and feeling like my face was on fire. I peered into the darkness, and the corners of my cramped tent gradually gave way to verdant foliage and soft hooting. I sat up and gaped into the trees at several large, shaggy figures a few meters away. The biggest of the three slowly raised his massive torso and turned toward me, his black, humanlike eyes glittering in the moonlight. *Holy shit.* I reached out my hand in a submissive greeting. All my training was about to be put to the test. *I won't let you down, Dian!* Rolling onto my stomach, I began a slow slither toward my new friend.

An overwhelming urge to vomit overtook my body, and the gorilla family receded from my foggy brain as I frantically yanked my tent zipper open and stumbled outside. It was pouring rain and, unable to stand, I crawled through the mud away from my tent and violently heaved up my dinner in the bushes. I rolled back into my tent and wrapped the sleeping bag around my shivering, boiling, muddy body. Piecing together my fever, vomiting, and hallucinations, I became convinced that I either was about to die of cerebral malaria or that my brain would boil, like Tim Robbins' in *Jacob's Ladder*. I thrashed around for the rest of the night, periodically expelling any food I had consumed over the past couple of days until I passed out from exhaustion.

The next day the baboons still were nowhere to be found, so we spent the afternoon relaxing on our cook Demekesh's porch. My fever had receded, but I was constantly sprinting up to the "toilet," a hole in the ground that Mat had dug. I eventually decided to simply stop eating—nothing in, nothing out.

"Not hungry? What you like?" Demekesh asked, her normally smiling face furrowed in concern. She offered to make me anything, and she was an excellent cook, but the thought of consuming solid food made my stomach roil.

"I'm not feeling well, Demi. I'll just make some tea, thank you."

"She's having DIARRHEA," Mat helpfully announced, translating this into broken Amharic to the entire camp.

Demi nodded sympathetically. A moment later, a big grin lit up her face, and she leapt up and hurried into her hut. She emerged a moment later with a nondescript bottle and gestured for me to scoot my blue-and-yellow plastic beach chair away from the wall. Perplexed but too tired to ask questions, I complied. Demi stood behind me, opened the bottle, and dumped the entire contents on my head. It was viscous and greasy, and she rubbed it into my scalp, saturating every follicle. I touched my hair, felt grease on my fingers, and recognized the familiar smell—olive oil.

"Much better," she said with a satisfied chuckle, giving my waist-length hair a final massage.

Much to everyone's surprise, my visits to the toilet continued unabated. The soft water of the hot springs did nothing to remove the grease from my hair. I put a towel on my pillow before bed, hoping the oil would absorb overnight.

The next morning I awoke with a slicked-back grease hairdo, and I was vomiting and sprinting to the toilet as usual. Mat took one look at my state of disrepair and finally decided I needed a doctor, so he, Demi, Teklu, and I loaded ourselves into the truck. We picked up several Afar men along the way who were eager to take advantage of a ride into Metahara. Their unsmiling faces, unblinking stares, and perpetually-misfiring Kalashnikov rifles usually unnerved me, but this time, fear of one of their guns going off in my face was subsumed by my attempts to keep my stomach inside my body as we careened along the rocky, sometimes-river, that constitutes the "road" to Metahara.

An hour later, I sat in a folding chair in a white concrete hospital building, listening to Teklu solemnly translate my symptoms to a roomful of curious nurses. Mat grinned sadistically, amused by the horror of the finer details of my bowel movements over the last few days.

One nurse, a petite woman in her early twenties, gestured for me to follow her outside. We rounded the path to an adjacent windowless building with three rusty metal doors. The nurse held out one piece of toilet paper and waved at the first door. With a growing sense of alarm, I reached my hand out to the sun-warmed, flaky metal handle and slowly creaked the door open.

The smell hit me first—the rotting poops of what seemed like all the sick people on Earth were emanating from a huge, reeking hole in the ground. Cobwebs sheathed the windowless walls, gargantuan insects writhing in their shadows. The nurse gestured at the piece of toilet paper again, smiled knowingly, and walked away.

I turned and wildly jogged up the path behind her, muttering in English that toilet paper was probably not the ideal medium for sample collection of this nature. She slipped inside a room around the corner and returned with a small wooden stick, which she placed firmly in my hand.

Armed with my paper and stick, perching precariously over hell's mouth, I attempted to create a sample and failed. After days of no food in and a million poops out, my body had had enough. And even if anything did come out, it wouldn't be the consistency to be captured successfully by a stick and sheet of toilet paper. The shame! After returning to the building and yelling "DIARRHEA!" repeatedly, I was finally given a plastic cup the size of a thimble, but it was too late, the sample collection was not happening. I was one of the few foreigners to visit the hospital, so a small crowd of fascinated and disgusted onlookers gathered to observe the plight of this pale, peeling, rashy, oily, human specimen of grotesqueness. I admitted unequivocal defeat and was told to return later when I was able to give the sample.

The rest of the day revolved around stuffing my face so I wouldn't fail my afternoon attempt. Back in Metahara, as I choked down forced mouthfuls of bread, Mat dialed his friend Steve, a skin doctor who visited us the week before, then thrust the phone at me.

"Hi, Steve? This is Vanessa. We met last week at Filoha. Thanks for prescribing me antibiotics for those festering leg sores, I appreciate it. Well, lately I've been having explosive diarrhea and puking my guts out, so Mat here was wondering what your thoughts are on that?"

Several hours later, I determinedly marched into the metal turd closet with my thimble. I finally produced a tiny sample, from which the doctor deduced that I had amoebic dysentery; my intestines were riddled with vicious little parasites that were burrowing into my insides and creating ulcers. The doctor prescribed antibiotics and sent me on my mortified way. Later, Mat was thoughtful enough to ask what my strategy was for getting the sample into the tube.

That night, I crawled into my filthy, damp tent, hoping to finally pass out. As I pulled up my sleeping bag, two gigantic, hairy spiders launched themselves directly at my face, eyes glittering. *Not tonight!!* I silently shrieked. My tent was a one-person unit roughly the size of a coffin—way too small for the three of us. I ninja-rolled out of the flap, grabbed a rock, and began wildly smashing. There was too much give on the tent walls, so I only managed to knock the spiders deep within my sleeping bag.

Exhausted and miserable, I rigged up a mosquito net under a tree and slept outside, listening to the bats crashing around the roof of Demi's hut, and the mice gnawing at Teklu's boots, and feeling massive insects dive-bombing the netting around me. At this point, the day somehow went from being awful to hilarious, and as much as I wanted a shower and toilet and bed, I was able to appreciate sleeping under the night sky full of twinkling stars, seeing the fireflies blinking, and hearing the hyenas softly laughing as I drifted off to sleep.

The dysentery initially improved but quickly returned to plague me for the remaining month. Strangely, I managed to get used to it; something about the peacefulness and beauty of the place distracted me. It was easier to cope while living outdoors as a member of a feral, turd-talking group of hooligans than it ever would have been in my comfortable, sterile apartment back home, surrounded by well-meaning normal people with nine-to-five jobs and a healthy aversion to repeated use of the word "diarrhea."

Vanessa Van Doren is a former wild baboon researcher, current medical student, and forever Masshole, currently living in Cleveland, Ohio. Her hobbies include drinking fancy beers, ranting about all the rashes and parasites she got in Ethiopia, and repeatedly failing to get into snow sports.

Because It Was a Sunday

Brazilian bush and fuzzy humpers.

IGUAZU FALLS ARE ONE OF THE NEW WONDERS OF THE World, but the Brazilian town that shares the name is a shithole. It is the Southern Hemisphere's answer to the American side of Niagara Falls: same overcast pallor, tacky keychains, unsavory characters, and general unease. I arrived here halfway through my great South American sojourn. The perception that Brazil is a land of sun-squinting beauty, voracious sexuality, and collective proficiency in thong-wearing, footballing, and dancing is accurate in many pockets of the country, just not in this pocket.

My friend Jess and I had crossed the continent to witness the majesty and magnitude of the falls, which were everything they were heralded to be. Trouble was, we had missed our departure bus and were marooned for an extra day in the moral vacuum of Foz do Iguaçu. Our purgatory hostel was, in its original incarnation, a psychiatric hospital. The place had yet to rid itself of the ominous smell of antiseptic or the trademark green linoleum flooring of mid-twentieth century institutions. It was still staffed by aging, disdainful nuns who appeared likely to restrain me to a cracked-leather gurney.

We'd shared a rough night's sleep, waking up every few hours to the sound of phantom phone calls and our curious mutual dream of hairless gray people lynching themselves with bed sheets. We stumbled out of the lobby and into the dying Sunday afternoon. Aggravated by hunger and the six-year-old guidebook my ever-thrifty father had gifted me, we walked the dusty streets and rough sidewalks looking for a meal. Everywhere we passed was closed or closing; gruff staff dragged outdoor tables inside and across the cracked, checkerboard tiles of restaurants.

Our patience with each other was becoming increasingly threadbare because of our circumstances. We weren't halfway to Sao Paulo, there were scowling nuns administrating our accommodations, our mouths were dry, and our search for food was fruitless. Adopting the tight jaws and crossed arms of enemies, we entered a hole in the wall that smelled distinctly of Brut cologne. Despite a slide letter board detailing all kinds of bastardized Italian and Greek dishes, we were told the only thing available was meat lasagna and Brahma beer. Why? Because it was Sunday.

Barring better judgment (and fearing MSG), I took a seat at one of the café's outdoor tables with my beer and the promise of lasagna. *Café* may sound charming. I assure you it was not. *Café* in itself is a stretch—no wine-bottle candleholders or flowers spilling out of terra cotta pots, no cobblestone streets or flamenco guitar for miles. The air hung heavy with humidity, neon lights hummed, and the table and chairs were cracked red plastic that pinched my legs whenever I squirmed. And squirm I did under the eye-fucking of the inexplicably tuxedoed waiter who in between Hoover-ing drags off his cigarette was readjusting his junk for our viewing pleasure. On any other day, in any other place, I would have left, but morale was low and I was hungry.

The beer was warm. The streets were empty save for the advancing sound of carnival music—a muffled serenade of stale funnel cakes and impending doom. I turned to see a single parade float crawling towards us, its perimeter bound by thick black prison bars. The makeshift cage held an obscene crowd of gyrating adults in matted furry costumes. Dingy magenta bunnies were grinding on tattered turquoise elephants, and there was a one-eyed fox bent under the defiling weight of a penguin whose right wing was clinging to the rest of its costume by a few strings. It was one of the strangest and most place-appropriate things I've ever seen. Then the float of degeneracy turned a street corner and vanished. Jess and I could do nothing but stare at each other, our eyes reflecting the same "Is this real?" sentiment.

The tuxedoed letch, unruffled by the parade, presented our lasagna: a plate of unboiled noodles layered with ketchup and granules of grey meat. For a country that exports more beef than anywhere else in the world, it seemed an affront to national identity. Losses were cut, lasagna was rejected, and beers were replenished.

Jess and I, trying to smooth the waters, traded questions about the personal lives of the *furries*: was it O.K. to copulate outside of your imagined species, or was is it a Noah's ark situation wherein foxes hunted for foxes and tigers for tigers; were there convenient zippers for exposing genitalia; was the fetish shamanistic in origin; what kind of dry cleaning bills were we talking; when you came out as furry, was it called coming out of the wilderness?

Just as we had started to ease the tension with tentative laughter, a short, dreadlocked man appeared next to us. He was not wholly unattractive. He kind of rocked a feral Christ-meets-*Taxi Driver* look. He had bare feet and spoke in broken English with extravagant hand gestures. From the smattering of rocks he poured onto our tabletop, I gathered he wanted to hustle some crystals. He used his fingers to push back his cheeks into the shape of a smile and stared expectantly at Jess, who, having reached her quota of local interaction for the evening, turned her back to him and assumed a don't-talk-to-me quasi-fetal position in her plastic chair. I (sufferer of chronic politeness) told him the stones were beautiful, but my friend and I were having a difficult day and were regrettably not interested in purchasing any of his wares. He bent down until his face was level with my own, pointed an oil-stained finger at me, and spat in the most searingly clear English I have ever heard, "You! Fuck you!" There aren't enough exclamation points to convey his fury. He turned and stomped away, cursing us in a menagerie of languages, the rough translation being that we were ugly, dog-fucking, lesbian prostitutes with big feet.

As I was waiting for Jess to deliver something—a hug, a commiseration of disbelief, a hallowed Fruit Roll-Up from her purse—she looked past me and whispered, "Keep your head down."

I heard it before I saw her: a high-pitched nasal mewl. She spewed desperate rapid-fire Portuguese. She pushed herself into my chair almost knocking me out of it. She smelled like smoke and was wearing Adidas rubber sandals, tie-front pajamas, and a stained wife beater. She sported a shock of Rod Stewart hair, a teardrop tattoo scratched into her cheek, and her eyes were like blue-flaming butane torches. She gave me the kind of stare you are trained not to return whether it is delivered by a wild animal or rabid human being, but I faltered and we locked eyes. If she was giving off a vibe it was static electric volts.

Jess shouted for the testicle jockey to bring us our check. Butane started stomping her feet and pointing at my wallet. I was about to hand her some Brazilian reals when she snatched my wallet out of my hands. Jess intervened throwing an elbow in the mix, freeing my wallet, and knocking the perpetrator backward. Butane responded by turning her face skywards and ripping off her clothes piece by piece.

First it was just the tank top, pulled over her head in a single graceful swoosh and then thrown into the street. Her bare chest vibrated with rage. Next to go were her pajama bottoms, untied and shaken off to display a spider web thigh-tattoo and an angry shock of bush a few inches from my face. It's the first and only time in my life that I've seen pubic hair wielded as a weapon in a holdup.

She was now equal parts stark naked and stark raving mad, dragging her bare feet on the concrete, pulling at her hair, and growling through impossibly white teeth. Our waiter, just a few feet away, leaned against the doorframe with an expression of shameless amusement. We jumped up from the table, threw some cash for whomever, and fled the scene.

As we ran through the now-dark street, I could feel the strain between Jess and me release. A derelict bush flasher, a crazy crystal pusher, and tainted ground meat will do that to a pair of broads. The evening's events had shown us both that if we wanted a friend in this godforsaken corner of the world, we were going to have to hold tight to each other—the big-footed, dog-fucking hookers that we were.

We went back the way we came, though now with arms wound protectively around each other. Trying to excavate a silver lining, I promised Jess that someday this night would become the story that made us laugh the hardest, the one we loved to tell the most. But right now, it was still too soon. I wanted a scouring shower, an ice cream cone with rainbow sprinkles, the sound of my mom's voice, and for the first time in a long time, I wanted to go home. We went back to our haunted hostel, turned on the bright lights, pushed our shitty hospital beds together, and waited for Monday.

Reda Wigle is a middle child named after a stigmatic saint. She likes bourbon and hates pants. Her favorite place is the one she hasn't seen yet.

ELIZABETH TASKER

The Chocolate
Egg Bomber

The scientist and the terrorist.

"WE RECOMMEND ALL FLIGHT PASSENGERS USE THE RESTROOM before boarding."

The last time someone had suggested this to me, I was out of nappies sufficiently recently not to be trusted on car journeys lasting more than 15 minutes. The consequences of avoiding such preparatory activities back then had led to the day my parents lovingly refer to as Brown Thursday, an event in which all defecating cattle in the local British countryside were upstaged by a toddler.

Now an astrophysicist in my mid-30s, it was rare that people questioned my continence. Japan Airlines clearly felt this was a grave omission. I thought this through. Then I went to the bathroom. Because there are some risks nobody should take.

It later transpired that the airline's true concern was the expected turbulence during the first part of the flight between Tokyo and Vietnam. Such air bumps meant that passengers would have to stay seated past the point when they would normally have relieved themselves, due to having chugged the giant bottle of Coke they couldn't bring through security. Thinking of which, I stopped by one of the terminal shops to pick up a drink for my own journey. Stacked invitingly in the refrigerator was a line of cola bottles, each and every one with "Good Luck" stamped on its label. I began to wonder if the universe was telling me something—such that I was about to sit beside a passenger whose hand luggage consisted of 36 Kinder Surprise chocolate eggs.

Had the gentleman in question been flying to the USA, he would never have made it past Customs and Border Protection. Comprised of a hollow milk chocolate shell with a toy in the center, these candy delights are known to kill American children on sight. So great is their lethal potency that attempting to bring these dangerous goods into the country will result in fines rumored to be between $300 and $2,500 *per* egg. This is even if you pack them snuggly between your entirely legal flamethrower, electric minigun, grenade launcher, and umbrella sword.

The eggs were stacked in their three-tier tray under my neighbor's seat. As I stepped carefully past him to take my own seat, I smiled and remarked jovially, "That is perhaps the most surprising hand luggage I've ever seen anyone bring!" I nodded toward the eggs.

The man said nothing.

Slowly, his head turned to stare silently back at me. Then his gaze returned without further acknowledgment to the back of the seat.

It was then I began to suspect he was going to kill us all. Remember the shoe bomber? That man packed his footwear with explosives and was only prevented destroying the plane by alert passengers and flight attendants. Now his memory was about to be entirely eclipsed by the guy who wired up his own detonation device from three dozen separate plastic parts embedded in milk chocolate goodness.

Of course, I was overreacting. The individual I had now silently labeled a threat to mankind may simply not have spoken English. He was a non-Asian on a flight between Japan and Vietnam who had just ordered his onboard drinks in English but it was perfectly possible that…no, it wasn't. He was clearly a terrorist.

The more I considered it (and I had a while on that delayed six-hour flight), the weirder it looked. After all, who brings large quantities of Italian chocolate from Japan to Vietnam? Given its intended recipients, why would you ever buy so much? The man was either a hardened criminal or the father of six sets of deprived American sextuplets who had been smuggled into Asia so they could finally experience the combined delight of a gift that was both a tooth-rotting snack and a toy with dangerously small parts. Both explanations would admittedly explain why he was at a loss for words.

I tried to watch a movie, but my eyes kept sliding toward the eggs. Innocent treats to melt in your mouth, or packed explosives to melt your plane? It was ridiculous, yet it smelled of genius. The eggs were supposed to have something inside them, so would it be detectable on the bag scanner if the contents were a toy or parts of an explosive device? If each egg were harmless separately, who would know the danger until they were connected together?

My neighbor's hand moved as he leaned forward. Mine twitched toward the flight attendant "help" button. But rather than reaching for the eggs, the man extracted the safety card from the seat pocket. Frankly, that was the most suspicious action yet: honestly, who reads that thing? Perhaps only someone who knew the plane was going down.

Part of me wanted to take a nap. The other part wanted to stay awake in case I had to save the world. It was a dilemma. The problem with dangerous ideas that are this absurd is that you know no one else is going to come up with them. This meant the guy had a clear run if I dozed off.

I decided to stay awake and vigilant. However, rather than announcing to the whole plane that we were all about to be murdered by chocolate eggs, I'd stay silent unless I saw:

The eggs suddenly connected together with wires.

The eggs being taken to the toilet.

Because seriously, the last one is abnormal *and* unhygienic.

The upshot was I kept half an eye on the eggs for most of the flight. My neighbor didn't use the bathroom; he had either followed the airline instructions before boarding the flight, or he had seen me staring at his candy and thought he would be down six eggs before he got back.

When we touched down safely in Hanoi, I concluded that it was my vigilance that had saved the day. I gave my flight companion a curt nod as I left; he knows what he did.

★

Elizabeth Tasker is an astrophysicist working in Japan. Originally from the UK, Elizabeth graduated from Durham University in theoretical physics before being inspired by Men in Black *and deciding to build parallel universes inside her computer. She therefore dropped south to Oxford and completed a doctorate in computational astrophysics. After that she moved, wandering minstrel style, to the USA and then to Canada on research positions, before taking up her current position in Japan. She now spends her days building galaxies in her computer and wondering when she will learn enough Japanese that the canteen will become less confusing than her research. Her popular science writing has appeared on sites that include* Scientific American, The Conversation, I Fucking Love Science, *and* Physics Focus, *and has received a collection of awards, including second prize in the 2014 Chemistry World science communication competition and first prize in the 2013 Global Voices from Japan column contest.*

GAZELLE PAULO

Friendly Skies

Coffee, tea, or Gaga?

Note from the Editor: You've probably heard about Gerard Depardieu urinating in the aisle of a plane. After reading about Depardieu's claims of drinking a case of wine a day, plus a half-bottle of pastis, some champagne, vodka, whiskey, and then the other half-bottle of pastis, I'm not surprised that he had a full bladder. You've probably seen outrageous behavior on planes, but can you imagine what a flight attendant sees over the course of a career? I wasn't sure I could envision the extent of it, so I asked Gazelle Paulo, a New York fashion writer, who is also a flight attendant, to reveal some of the weirdest things he's experienced on a plane.

★

I HAVE BEEN WORKING AS A FLIGHT ATTENDANT FOR OVER seventeen years at a major U.S. airline, and I love it. But dealing with the public is not an easy task, and if you are 33,000 feet above the ground, the solution to a problem is not always within arm's reach.

Stars in the Sky—Celebrities!

Flight crews have incredible access to celebrities in the premium cabins. I have had the pleasure of seeing and meeting so many world icons that I'm just not bothered anymore, until they're a bother, that is. I do admit I was star-struck when Faye Dunaway was on my flight from Paris to New York. She was the last person to board the plane, arriving about ten minutes after the scheduled departure time. She didn't have a personal entourage, but the airport service attendants were helping to carry her six Louis Vuitton duffel bags, which I had to find space for on a full flight. I'm not complaining. I love my job.

But when it comes to entourage, or assistants, Madonna is a mile high above the rest. On a flight from New York to Sao Paulo, Madonna was the last to board the flight. She was escorted right up to the airplane door by someone pushing a trolley cart with her carry-on. She was the vision of a material girl. But this was the special part: she sat in first class with an assistant who was in charge of preparing her special meal in the galley. Madonna's special meal came with an assistant.

> EDITOR: Now that's special. What did Madonna's special-meal assistant prepare?
>
> GAZELLE: It was a mix of vegetables that needed to be left in the oven for a specific time.
>
> EDITOR: Was Madonna wearing pants? I still haven't recovered from seeing her bare butt getup at the Grammy Awards.
>
> GAZELLE: She was wearing sweat pants; very simple. The grandeur of the moment came with all the entourage surrounding her.

I wish I could leak the name of *The Usual Suspects* actor who (on a flight from London to New York) told the purser not to speak to him during the rest of the flight. The American actor shouted "Leave me alone!" so rudely that the word "rude" is too civil to use as a description.

> EDITOR: Gazelle, I'm sorry to interrupt, but this isn't fair. We need to know who. Maybe you can give us a hint. According to IMDb, Kevin Spacey auditioned for *The Gong Show* twice in the seventies and was rejected both times. So, just ring the gong once if it was Kevin Spacey who yelled at the purser.

> GAZELLE: Well, unfortunately I can't. Just thinking about it gives me chills and I am afraid nightmares could affect the peace of my Brazilian/ *American Beauty* state of mind....

> EDITOR: Please tell me it wasn't Benicio del Toro. He's so nice in my fantasies.

> GAZELLE: With those eyes, I don't think Benicio could ever be rude to anybody.

Lady Gaga is on the Jet Bridge

The queen of the little monsters takes her fashion image so seriously that she risks breaking her ankles and holding up flights in the name of style. I'd finished welcoming all the passengers aboard a flight from London to New York when I saw Lady Gaga (being escorted by airport security and followed by her entourage) coming my way down the jet bridge. She was walking on skyscraper-tall platform shoes with no heels. As she entered the inclined jet bridge she decided to walk sideways to avoid falling, touching the walls with her two hands, while her entourage and airline staff followed her tottering progress. It took her about 15 minutes to inch her way down a ramp which is a normal 30-second jaunt.

> EDITOR: So next time our readers are sitting aboard their flights, delayed at the gate, wondering if they're going to make their connections, it could be because a celebrity is holding up departure due to wearing stupid shoes?

> GAZELLE: Well, I wanted to shout, "take off the shoes for God's sake!" since there were no paparazzi or *Fashion Police* members around to document that silly scene.

> EDITOR: Do pilots ever say, "Screw you Lady Gaga. This plane is outta here."?

> GAZELLE: They had no idea what was going on; only me, gate agents and Gaga's entourage witnessed that. Come to think of it, she could write the song "My Shoes Are Too Sexy for This Jet Bridge."

> EDITOR: Was the rude actor from *The Usual Suspects* Kevin Spacey?

> GAZELLE: Don't interrupt me, honey, when I am talking about Gaga's shoes.

I Am too Big for this Door

On a 757 from New York to San Juan, a large man entered the aft lavatory, and the door closed snuggly behind him. But due to his size he couldn't turn around to open the door, nor could he reach behind himself to slide it open. He was stuck. Then he panicked. He started screaming at the top of his lungs. We couldn't open the door for him because he was wedged against it, sealing it shut. We finally got the tools and removed the entire door. The screeching man backed out and returned to his seat.

> EDITOR: I was just thinking that Alec Baldwin was hauled off an American Airlines flight a few years ago for having a tantrum after being asked to turn off his phone. His brother Stephen was in *The Usual Suspects*. Was Stephen Baldwin the actor who yelled at the purser?

> GAZELLE: Alec Baldwin could yell at the purser, at the whole cabin crew, at me, even at Lady Gaga...he is so cute.

I Am Too Big for this Toilet Seat

Our plane was circling the skies around JFK Airport. We couldn't land because one of our passengers was seated, but not in her seat. She was on the toilet seat, panties down, and she couldn't get up. Three acrobatic flight attendants couldn't budge the bulging woman from the bitty bathroom. The plane kept circling. There wasn't space for the cabin crew to squish behind her to get leverage. The plane kept circling. The woman's legs tired from her valiant effort. We coaxed and coached her. Then finally with a final burst of willpower, she pushed, and grunted and strained, and we freed her.

> EDITOR: Gazelle, even Disney realized they had to do something about the It's a Small World ride when the ever-fattening theme park attendees were bottoming out the boats. People were lighter in the '60s when the ride was designed. But it seems the airlines aren't getting this and

everything on board is shrinking while the population's girth is expanding. Please don't tell me that the seats aren't getting smaller, because that means I'm getting bigger.

GAZELLE: Sorry to inform, but you are getting bigger.

EDITOR: Kevin Pollak was in *The Usual Suspects* but I just can't picture him yelling at the purser, and Gabriel Byrne is from Dublin, and Pete Postlethwaite was born in Cheshire. Was it Chazz Palminteri or Kevin Pollak who was rude?

GAZELLE: Do you ever give up on something?

What's Love Got to Do with It?

The airplane front door was closed, and we were still parked at the gate while the last of the cargo was loaded. So we decided to take the dinner preferences on this London-to-New York flight. When I reached the last row, a "gentleman" punched a woman's face, and then she returned a punch to his face. Oh Lord have mercy on me! After a nanosecond of shock, I told them both to hold onto those thoughts, and I ran to first class to get the purser. By the time we came back, the couple looked like the Ike and Tina Turner characters in their biographic movie *What's Love Got to Do With It*. The door was reopened and we left without them.

No First-Time Ambien on a Plane

A gentleman, seated in business class on a flight to Rio de Janeiro, decided to take a "few Ambiens" after dinner service and lights were out so he could fall asleep. A few hours later, in the dark, he was completely naked walking in between cabins. The crew spotted his white ass and took him to his seat, but he was naked and didn't remember where he'd left his clothes. He stayed naked in his seat, under a blanket, until we landed in Rio. After all passengers deplaned we were able to find his ensemble, which was neatly placed in an overhead bin in the main cabin.

Just No Ambien, Please!

On another flight to Rio, also in business class, a naked lady (naked except for her pink socks with daisy prints) decided to go to the first row of the cabin in the middle of the night, turned her back to the division partition, and right there she took a dump. We, the cabin crew, believed that she thought she was in her bathroom because she tried to reach for invisible toilet paper and touched a sleeping passenger's leg. The poor guy woke to find that the floor and his shoes were covered in shit. We wrapped the woman in a clean blanket while we carefully tried to wake her up—many times—and after we succeeded and explained the situation to her, she was so distressed and embarrassed that she asked to be moved to a seat in the back of the main cabin, where she stayed until the end of the flight. The gentleman whose shoes she defecated upon deplaned only wearing his socks.

Phlegm au Poivre

In the middle of the first-class dinner service enroute to Buenos Aires, a gentleman fell asleep right after I put his plate of steak au poivre on his tray table. His head was tilted forward, and as he was snoring a cascade of mucus was pouring out of his nose, over his shirt, and onto his plate. It was a dilemma. I knew I had to let him know. I wasn't sure how to delicately handle this snot issue. So I decided to go back to the galley to get some hot towels to give him upon waking. It took a while for the galley flight attendant to find some extra towels since we had used most of them right before the beginning of the service. When I returned to the passenger with the moist hot towels, he was awake and attacking his phlegm-sauce steak. His shirt was still slick with snot. Should I have said something?

> EDITOR: Gazelle, was Kevin Spacey the actor who shouted "Leave me alone!"?

> GAZELLE: Oh my God, would YOU just please leave me alone!

★

Gazelle Paulo, 45, is a Brazilian-born international flight attendant based out of JFK Airport. Gazelle has been flying for over seventeen years—mostly between U.S. and South America/Europe—for one of the biggest American commercial carriers in the world, but nonetheless he has traveled all over the world. His favorite routes are from New York to Rome, Rio de Janeiro, and Brussels. Besides flying, Gazelle is a fashion observer for The-Blot Magazine. *@gazellepaulo*

SHANNON BRADFORD

The Córdoban Crap

"Ooh, but I still smell her."
—*Lt. Col. Frank Slade,* Scent of a Woman

I USE POSITIVE AND WELL-TIMED BATHROOM VISITS AS PER-haps the number one barometer of trip success. I've had plenty of diarrhea-fraught explorations through Central America, a few close calls in Europe, and a good number of bidet bloopers in the Middle East. But on this par-ticular trip (two months backpacking through Argentina, Bolivia, and Peru), I had been nailing the pee-and-poo visits like an old pro. You wouldn't catch me in a bath-room without my purse toilet paper, nor squeezing my thighs on a street corner. I was an efficient urinating-and-pooping machine.

My boyfriend Jorge and I cruised into Córdoba, Argen-tina, to stay with a friend for a few days. We were planning on doing the tourist thing before swinging north and then crossing into Bolivia. We skipped arm in arm through the parks with the doves and the children, gawked at cathe-drals, meandered along sidewalks, and fingered expensive clothing we would never buy. We drank gallons of Malbec and ate megatons of bread.

Then one particular morning in the miniscule apartment of Jorge's friend, I felt a rumbling in my belly. Miguel, the friend, had gone to work, leaving my boyfriend and me in the two-room apartment. We were sharing a twin bed that doubled as a couch in the main area that was also the kitchen, living room, and dining room. Bodily function planning was necessary here too because peeing in the middle of the night meant awkward moments, as the only way to the bathroom was through the bedroom of our sleeping host.

The rumble promised to be interesting, as my schedule had been thrown off by the high bread/meat-to-fiber ratio (also known as the Argentinian Diet), something a bit outside my regular eating lifestyle. In fact, it was less of a rumble and more of a surprise punch in my lower abdomen, followed by several seconds of intense, possibly perforating intestinal pain and then a distinct need to let the monster out right then. I hightailed it to the bathroom (approximately five feet away) and had a relieving, if somewhat strenuous and painful evacuation experience.

Per standard bathroom protocol, I turned to behold my triumph. The accomplishment that greeted me was obscenely large. My intestines tend to do that while traveling—produce Guinness Book of World Record-style shits that both baffle and amaze. I congratulated myself as I flushed Jabba-the-Turd down the drain. And then I flushed it again because it had stubbornly reappeared in the hole. And then, again. This poop protégé seemed really curious about the outside world. One more flush. Still there, eyeing me. Knowing.

Somewhere in the tomes of time there is written the Five Flush Maximum. No one knows if that's when suspicions of nearby people are finally raised, or if that's when the toilet water level stops replenishing itself out of defiance, but that's when I gave up. The log refused to disappear.

There was a swirl of panic within me—leaving a very obvious and obscenely large loaf of dung in a host's bathroom is one of the things you aren't supposed to do as an appreciative guest. Luckily there was no line of people waiting outside or group of people within hearing of every fart and sigh, two situations I'd been in before. Only Jorge, my boyfriend, waited outside, and he was more than accustomed to what came out of my ass.

Nonetheless, I couldn't leave this thing here. We had to get rid of it. "Honey?" I called my extremely hesitant boyfriend into the bathroom. He nearly gagged when he saw the issue at hand. "Can you help me?"

He looked like he wanted to say no, but instead moved toward the toilet. I left him to work on the problem. He emerged from the bathroom a while later, looking frazzled.

"It won't go down," he said, "and there's no plunger."

"Well, we can't leave it there." I checked my watch. "We have three hours until Miguel is back. Let's go buy a plunger. Why doesn't he have a plunger?"

"Most people don't poop like you," he pointed out.

"Yeah, well, it's just one of those things. Every house should have a plunger." I'd come up against this frustrating aspect of life many times. The fear of the mega-shit lurked when I was away from my own bathroom. Not everybody has industrial strength toilets. Miguel didn't. Although everyone knows it happens to all of us, there is something embarrassing about bodily functions. It's an avoid-their-phone-calls-and-never-see-them-again type of embarrassment, especially when the bodily function leaves such a large and smelly footprint.

Furthermore, this was a friend of my boyfriend, a man I'd met two days ago. I was supposed to impress him but not with the size of my shit. This wasn't the parting gift I'd intended to leave.

So we began the plunger search. Jorge and I hit the pavement, both of us agitated in our own ways—me, because of the discarded fragment of an ass tree trunk, and Jorge (probably) because he'd had to both smell it and look at it.

Two blocks turned into five, which turned into eight, which turned into ten. We walked 15 blocks to find one supermarket that sold things that could quite possibly include a plunger. We burst through the shop's doors, reinvigorated with hope. Miguel was due home in just over an hour. Time was running out.

We found a very tiny and long-neglected home goods section. Brooms, dustpans, latex gloves, cleaning implements—score! The section was badly organized and looked like workers had stocked its shelves by throwing the items toward the area from the storage room. I had to search the area a few times. It didn't include a plunger. Just as we resigned ourselves to the fact that plungers don't exist in Córdoba—we spotted a suction cup. Upon closer inspection, it turned out to be the suction cup that is usually part of a plunger, except without the stick part. And there was only one.

I snatched it up, positive that my farmhand boyfriend could figure out a way to utilize this thing. We strolled to the register confident, knowing that my very large and very stubborn embarrassment was soon to be a memory for just the two of us.

At the register, I added a candy bar. The woman scanned the candy, set it aside, and then spent a lot of time examining the suction cup. Finally, she looked at us and said, "I can't sell this to you."

The words barely made sense to me. "You…you can't?"

She shook her head. "There's no bar code."

I looked at Jorge, at the suction cup, back toward where we'd found it, and then at the lady. "But we found it over there…I mean, it's for sale. Can't you just…?"

The cashier shook her head and placed the would-be plunger to the side.

"But what are you going to do with it? You can't sell it. Why can't we just have it? What are you going to do, throw it away?"

By this time, Jorge was clearing his throat in a way that signaled I should shut up and was jabbing me impatiently in my lower back. The cashier offered one last unhelpful smile, took my money for the candy, and we left the store in a grim cloud.

Back at Miguel's house, we improvised a plan in a rapidly shriveling window of time. We'd scour the house one last time. We'd find a plastic bottle, and make a siphon of some sort. Yeah, that should work. And maybe he had some sacrifice-able silverware somewhere to use as surgical tools.

Somehow this shit was going down.

The bathroom was undeniably smelly, like something dead that had been out in the sun too long. After several thorough searches through the apartment, we found nothing useful to help with the mission. Jorge and I stared—grimaced, really—into the toilet, wondering what to do.

"We need to break it somehow," I suggested, feeling a little lightheaded from the smell.

Jorge was silent as he mulled more options. I knew his problem-solving wheels were turning, and I was confident he'd come up with an ingenious solution.

Finally, he left the bathroom without a word, rummaged in the kitchen, and reappeared with a plastic shopping bag.

He handed it to me. "Tie it onto my hand." He offered his hand like a resigned patient offering over the limb to be amputated.

"Are you serious?"

He nodded solemnly, eyeing the toilet. "It's the only way."

I tied the plastic bag to his hand, not just a little bit amazed. He looked queasy.

"Jorge," I said, "You don't have to do this…"

He shook his head. "It's O.K. I'll just try to break it up."

I watched as he neared the toilet, the dour look on his face mutating into something I'd never seen before and have never seen since—a combination of dread and resignation, like this were a paper shredder he was about to stick his hand into, and not just a clogged toilet.

I stepped out of the bathroom before his hand touched the water. Really, it was more for his sake than mine. My boyfriend had pulled the hero card, and I was biting back disbelieving giggles and terrified shrieks. Besides, the moment deserved some sanctity, or at least respectful silence, not ear-piercing howls in his eardrum.

I paced Miguel's tiny bedroom anxiously, waiting for something, anything. What would come of a grown man sticking his barely-protected hand into a toilet bowel full of intestinal debris? I didn't know.

"Did it work?" Several interminable moments had passed and I tried to sound extra cheerful, as though this were totally commonplace.

He didn't answer. Then there was a cough, and Jorge emerged from the bathroom as though he were leaping from the window of a burning house.

"I almost puked," he said, burying his head into the crook of his elbow.

His plastic bagged hand held a suspicious lack of something, though I didn't know what I had been expecting—the sacred tree trunk itself?

After he'd recovered enough, he bolted for the kitchen, shedding the plastic bag delicately yet quickly. He threw it into another plastic bag, tied the clean one tight, and then threw it into the trash like it was evidence to be destroyed.

"I touched it," Jorge said. "I actually felt it." And then he shuddered.

I watched him with a mixture of awe and disbelief. Had this man really volunteered to stick his hand in a toilet where the sure outcome was to touch his girlfriend's shit? I choked back another hysterical gobble of laughter, unsure whether now was the time to congratulate him or send him to therapy.

"Did it go down?"

He shook his head, still looking like someone in the throes of PTSD. "No, it's still there."

I groaned. "Shit! Well what are we gonna do? Miguel will be home any minute."

Jorge exhaled deeply, his face resuming a more normal color.

"We should leave the apartment," I said. "Like, right now. Come on, let's go buy the bus tickets for the north, which we need to get today anyway. We don't want to be here when he sees it."

"O.K. Let's go now. And we'll take out the trash on our way."

Jorge and I made it out of the house before Miguel got back, headed for the bus terminal wondering about what might transpire in our absence. "What a horrible surprise," I lamented. It would be one thing if the poop were anywhere near normal. There still existed the distinct possibility that it might never flush at all.

We spent a few hours in the terminal, wandering the endless rows of bus company stalls, and then returned to the apartment. Miguel was sitting at his dining room table, thumbing through a magazine.

"Hey guys," he said. "How was your day?"

I froze, so said nothing. Jorge played the cool guy part, and they talked for a bit about how work had gone, our bus ticket prices, our midday wanderings. He left out any mention of crazed plunger searches and touching my poo.

As they spoke I headed innocently to the bathroom but was reluctant to enter. I had to. What if Miguel had stopped off to pee right away, like most normal human beings did when they got home? What if he'd seen it? What if—I stopped myself there. The sordid, smelly truth awaited me. I entered the bathroom. I lifted the toilet lid. Clear water sparkled back at me. I blinked hard and looked closer. No peeking poop log; no Andean mountain of toilet paper; no skid marks. It was completely clean. Thoroughly puzzled, I sat down to pee, letting my gaze wander as I mulled over the strange turn of events. Then my eyes caught something suspiciously familiar near to the sink base—a rubber suction cup. Except this one had a stick attached. Sitting out where it very clearly had not been hours before, and still moist from what I can only assume was a marathon and near fatal plunging session. My head dropped to my hands and I screamed silently, mortified. Miguel had plunged my monster crap, and worse yet, he had the plunger in the house the whole time. Where it had been, we'll never know.

I walked back into the main room, trying but failing to hide the shock and bemusement from my face. Jorge caught on right away. When Miguel received a call and moved to his bedroom, I told Jorge the sad truth. "The poop is gone." I put my hand on his shoulder. "He had a plunger the whole time."

Jorge looked at me like this was some sort of cruel joke.

"I'm serious. Do you know what this means?"

He sighed and placed his forehead against my arm. "Yes."

"You touched my poo and you didn't even have to."

★

Shannon Bradford is 20-something years old and has a fondness for outdoor markets, ancient ruins, and foreign tongues (as in languages). A native of northern Ohio, she is currently living in South America with her Argentinian partner, a detail she uses to justify her degree in Latin American literature. Her days are spent writing, mastering Spanish, and learning the ins and outs of the expatriate lifestyle.

My Night in a
Shipping Container

Kuala Lumpur to Nigeria, delivery not guaranteed.

MY WIFE WAS GONE WHEN I WOKE UP. SHE HAD WRITTEN ME a note. "Happy birthday!" it said. "Pack what you'll need for the weekend. Meet me at the airport at 4:00. Don't forget your passport."

We had been living in Singapore for two-and-a-half months. We hadn't yet had time to take advantage of all the budget flights around Asia one finds here. Where Kattina was taking me was a secret, and "Don't forget your passport" was hardly a clue. In an island nation just twenty-six miles across, there's no such thing as a domestic flight.

So in the afternoon I hopped the subway to the airport. Kattina was waiting with two tickets to Kuala Lumpur. We were both excited as our flight touched down in Malaysia's capital, a little after sunset. "I found us a guesthouse online," Kattina said as we bussed into downtown. "It looks cute. I got us a courtyard room."

A courtyard room? That sounded nice.

Kattina and I like to think of ourselves as flexible and adventurous travelers. Accommodations aren't where we normally splurge. Non-fancy rooms mean we can afford more nights in exciting places. But, O.K., it was my birthday. Why not live it up a little in a "courtyard room"?

At first glance, the 41 Berangan Guesthouse seemed like our kind of place. "Snug, Safe, and Quirky!" cried a stack of brochures on the reception desk. "Spanking clean and fresh, 41 Berangan cheerily sits round the corner from all trappings of Kuala Lumpur's must-do's.... Snuggly comfy beds let you dream—*berangan*—away!"

Quirky! Snuggly! At 130 ringgit (U.S. $40) a night, I was sold.

"Please pay now," the receptionist said.

I'm an experienced world explorer, an international tour guide and travel writer, a guy who has been ripped off in enough countries to know better than to blindly hand over my credit card before seeing a room. But, I dunno, I guess I was distracted by thoughts of imminent birthday gifts.

"Of course we'll pay now," I smiled. I signed the bill, and the receptionist led us to our snuggly, quirky, courtyard room.

If you ever want to design a courtyard, 41-Berangan-style, here is how you do it: find a concrete building with two exterior walls at a right angle to each other. Place a shipping container to form a second right angle with one of those walls. Then complete a square with another shipping container so everything is boxed in. Add a picnic table and a couple of potted palms, and *voilà!* Instant courtyard! As an added bonus, you now have two shipping container rooms that, if needed, are easy to transport during the night.

I don't know about you, but when I think of sleeping in shipping containers, I think of human trafficking and dead refugees. Our courtyard "room" had a padlock on the outside of the door, which did not assuage these concerns. But, hey, I thought, we're flexible and adventurous travelers. Two nights in a shipping container would be...quirky!

It was a standard-sized shipping container with a bed, a small writing desk, and a retrofitted wall that separated a bathroom from the sleeping area. If I left the container door open, I had a view of the courtyard, not to mention that safe, secure, snuggly feeling one gets knowing one will not be padlocked in from the outside and shipped to Nigeria during the night. Even when we closed the door—for privacy and because we thought a one-way ticket to Lagos might be interesting—we still had a view of sorts. A little window gazed out at a concrete wall six inches away. So, really, the place was lovely. There was even carpeting!

Now, snooty cultural perfectionists might say, "Yeah, right. You can't carpet a shipping container. It ruins the authenticity." But the guesthouse owners at the 41 Berangan had thought of *everything* to create just the right ambiance. To make things rustic, the carpeting they installed had a faded appearance and musty aroma that created the sensation of sleeping in a shipping container that, at one point, had been dumped in the ocean.

Kattina grimaced. "Do you want to stay here?"

To be honest, I did not. Because, although I am a flexible and adventurous traveler, and this shipping container seemed pretty exciting, I wanted to splurge, pay the extra ten ringgit and upgrade to a "superior" room. What luxuries might await us there? A Jacuzzi? A minibar with rohypnol-enhanced beverages? The possibilities were endless.

We went back to the reception.

"Sorry," the receptionist said. "Our superior rooms are fully booked. Maybe tomorrow."

We returned to our shipping container.

"Do you *really* want to stay here?" Kattina asked.

We discussed our options. We had already paid. It was too late in the evening for the guesthouse to sell the room to someone else, so they weren't going to give us a refund. Besides, friends were waiting to meet us for dinner. And while I really wanted to see if we might find a place down the road where we could sleep in a cardboard box, or a retrofitted fridge, we just didn't have time to look.

"We should stay," I said. "We are flexible and adventurous travelers."

We didn't spend much time in our shipping container that evening. We went out to celebrate my birthday and to consume enough adult beverages that we would be able to sleep later. We were unsuccessful in the latter of the two endeavors. I laid awake most of the night, buzzing with anticipation of the crane that would come and lift us *berangan!*—away!

But luck was not with us. Our crane never came. We awoke in the morning, still in Kuala Lumpur. On our second night, we upgraded.

For those ten extra ringgit, we got a less exciting room in the main building. It had a television, and a DVD player, and a stack of pirated DVDs, which were nice and all, but the room did not have the mold-scented air freshener that came with our shipping container, nor did it give us that special feeling of rugged adventure we seek in foreign lands.

So if you happen to be visiting Malaysia's capital, and you stay at the 41 Berangan, be sure to request a courtyard room. And if you should have better luck than Kattina and I did, please send us a postcard from Nigeria.

★

Dave Fox is founder of the Globejotting.com global storytelling website. He teaches online humor and travel writing courses and has written two bestselling travel books—Globejotting: How to Write Extraordinary Travel Journals *and* Getting Lost: Mishaps of an Accidental Nomad. *Originally from the United States, Dave now lives in Vietnam and writes extensively about Southeast Asia.*

JON PENFOLD

A Bad Day

*The author goes on a 7,000-mile bike ride across the
USA for no reason.*

A BAD DAY STARTS WITH A HANGOVER—A POUNDING OF THE
head, like a child throwing a rubber ball against your front
door, except this annoying brat cannot be shooed away.
*Boom...boom...boom...*it repeats itself, in case you didn't
get it the first time."I am inside your skull," it declares over
and over,"in that space between bone and brain, and I will
only escape with time and only when I feel that the time
is right." *Boom... boom...boom...*

Returning to sleep seems to be the logical thing to do.
Close your eyes, Jon, try to ignore your wandering mind,
the spliced memories of the night before, the montage
of regret. But it's not that simple. There is no mute button, and the soundtrack loops with unlikely instruments:
jackhammers and hand grenades. Bury your head in the
crumpled-up rain jacket, press your palms against your
temples, and talk to yourself in the third person, Jon. But
still, *boom...boom...boom...*

It gets hotter by the minute. The warm summer sun
beats down on the thin plastic of a one-person tent,
heating the stagnant air inside. Your lungs long for cool,

refreshing oxygen, not the carbon-dioxide coffin that makes you feel like a sumo wrestler trapped in a sauna. Sweat bubbles on your skin, dampening the down sleeping bag into a moisture cocoon that you are responsible for creating. Time to get up, Jon, crawl from the cave and return to the first person.

I stand up and stretch my arms toward the heavens, except today I seriously doubt any existence of an afterlife. In fact, if there is a god, she can go fuck herself. It is an hour before noon and my morning is shot. Bright light pierces through the slits of my eyelids, penetrating my corneas and irises, sending a radioactive shock through my mind. I take a swig of water and immediately it throws itself in reverse, returning on the same course it went down. Taking down my tent has never seemed so complicated, packing my belongings has never been such a frustrating event, like trying to force the square block through the circle cutout. Finally it's time to ride and still, *boom…boom…boom…*

The pavement might as well be wet concrete and I'm dragging a cinder block through the gray mess. Declines become straightaways, straightaways become hills, hills become mountains. I am the Sherpa and the hangover laughs at my struggle. Drooped over the handlebars, my ass off the saddle, I climb but feel as if I'm going nowhere.

It's late May but the sun pounds with the hell-driven force of mid-August. Like a crooked judge I sentence innocent water into the prison that is my body. But only moments after the incarceration begins, there is a mass breakout, a thousand drops of sweat burrowing through my skin, my hair follicles their escape route, pouring from the mop of my head, the bush of my armpits, the rainforest of my crotch. Soon I am drenched, as if I have taken a shower fully clothed.

Then the noise starts, a high-pitched squall that pierces my ears like a rusted drill into tooth decay, like a picnic beneath an electric line. At first I am confused. What the hell is making this god-awful sound? Is it a turbine engine with a cracked valve? Perhaps it's the rusted steam whistle of an early locomotive? Maybe a loose fan belt in a 1983 Cadillac Coupe de Ville? Or an alarm, warning society that Russia has finally pushed the button, unloading a blitzkrieg of nukes on the United States? No, I realize that it can't be any of those things, because it's not isolated. The disturbance is not coming from a single source. The sound is everywhere—to the left and to the right, up and down, in front and behind. Something in my mind clicks, a flash-back from tenth-grade biology class, and I realize nature is to blame. "*EEEEEEEEEEEEE,*" they scream.

I can't see the culprits; they hide in the woods, hanging from tree branches, crawling up bark, longing for the sky. They are known in some parts of the world as "jar flies," the locals call them "dry flies," and oftentimes they are mistakenly referred to as "locusts," but they are cicadas. They have large eyes, wide apart, and transparent wings with visible veins. They don't bite or sting, but can be as annoying and troublesome as any insect that does. Their disturbance is their sound and their sound is my plight, and it only helps to amplify the banging in my head. *EEEEEEEEEEEEEEEEEEE...boom...boom...boom... EEEEEEEEEEEEEEEEE...*

This noise, this nearly intolerable nature cry, is commonly referred to as the "cicada song." And though it may sound slightly more pleasant than a Japanese man singing karaoke in an airport lounge, it contains no melody or rhythm and by no means holds any musical qualities. Unlike the grasshopper or cricket, which make noise by rubbing its legs and wings together, the cicada vibrates its tymbals: membrane-like structures on its nearly hollow air-filled belly. It is only the male cicadas that discharge this wailing noise as a mating call. And though I can completely understand the desire to get laid, the "song" only magnifies the violent misery in my head. *EEEEEEEEEEEEEE… boom…boom…boom…EEEEEEEEEEEEEE…*

I'm dog-tired but I've only been riding for about an hour. On any other day I would pull to the side of the road and lie down beneath a large tree in the cool shade of an overhanging canopy of leaves. But today there is no choice. There is a corkscrew-driving pain in the center of my skull, an alcohol-induced virus reprogramming the computer in my brain. It tells me to go on, to keep pushing out of the woods and away from the cicadas' "song."

I am barely paying attention to my surroundings, but suddenly I realize that the noise has faded, dissolving in the void I have left behind, becoming fainter with every pedal stroke. I cruise into a small Tennessee town without even realizing that I had crossed the state line. For the first time on my journey I welcome the sounds of civilization: the beeps, clanks, and *rat-a-tat-tats* of automobiles, the bangs, pops, and thuds of industry, the groans, moans, and shrieks of society.

I pull into a supermarket with the belief that adding some food to my stomach will replenish my energy. What is normally one of my favorite parts of the day suddenly becomes a frustrating dilemma, a battle between mind and body. I think I'm hungry but have no appetite. I roam the store, staring blankly at shelves and coolers and freezers chock-full of every kind of food imaginable. And though I know what I like, I haven't the slightest idea of what I want. Nothing looks appealing, so I settle on a container of store-made macaroni salad, hoping that the carbohydrate packed noodles will give me a much-needed boost.

As soon as I step out of the store, I wolf down the macaroni salad without so much as tasting it. My tongue, just the same as the rest of my body, still hasn't recovered from the substance abuse it endured the night before:

cigarettes, beer, women, whiskey, and such. If not for the texture, it could just as well have been dog food that I shoveled down my throat. My taste buds wouldn't have noticed the difference.

It's Friday of the Memorial Day weekend and traffic in town builds with workers getting out early and families on the move. I hit red light after red light, never settling into any sort of rhythm. I receive dirty looks, honks, and needless language shouted from open car windows, as if for some reason it is solely my fault that the streets are gridlocked, that somehow a lone bicyclist is to blame for a million pounds of steel moving as slow as sap on a cold day.

I make it to the west side of town and the discomfort in my head journeys south through my body. It transforms into a gurgle in my throat and a clawing at the inner smokestack of my windpipe. Then it works its way into the chest, a slow burn surrounding the blood-pumping factory that is my heart. Finally it arrives in the stomach as a churning, curdling rot-machine, grinding away at the linings of my gut. Then instantly, without the courtesy of even asking, it decides that it's coming back up.

I pull to the side of the road, hop off my bike, and bend over. My palms against my knees, my chin at my chest, I let my body do what it wants. The contents of my stomach project from my mouth like water from a fire hose. I paint the earth at my feet an off-white. Macaroni shells are splattered throughout the puddle. I dry heave with drool hanging from my lower lip. My stomach makes certain that it is empty. I look closely at the ground and realize the mess doesn't look any different than when it was prepackaged at the market. Did I even attempt to chew the noodles? As I straighten back up and walk toward my bike, I consider the lesson that I just learned: perhaps when hung over and exerting physical force on a near hundred-degree day, consuming anything that contains a mayonnaise base is not the best of ideas.

I feel better now. My head has cleared, as well as my stomach, though I continue to sweat profusely. I have made it out of town and am pedaling at a nice pace. I stop at a small country store and purchase a couple of sports drinks, pounding back one of them before I make it out the door. I tuck the other one away in my bag and consult a map of Tennessee. The road that I'm on appears to circle northwest, miles above a large lake, forming an arch-shaped line on the paper. Directly to my left though, there is a road that is not on the map. The road to the left appears to go straight, just above the lake, which according to my shoddy calculations would cut off a good ten miles and save me about an hour. A shortcut! But why isn't it on the map? Because if it was on the map, then it wouldn't be a shortcut.

I swing left. Million-dollar homes climb out of green hills on both sides of the road. I pass a country club, its parking lot filled with Cadillacs, BMWs, and Mercedes Benzes, its greens crowded with doctors, lawyers, and trust-fund babies. As for golf, Mark Twain once referred to it as "a good walk ruined," and I couldn't agree more. But on this day I am glad to see the course, because after all, these links *must* be the reason this road is not on the map: so its wealthy members don't have to deal with us commoners passing through their manmade paradise.

I see the lake on my left, blue and choppy, motorboats pulling water skiers in circles. I appear to be on the right path when abruptly the paved road turns narrow—one dusty lane. The green hills evolve into thick woods with jumbled trees, their leaves blocking the sun. Million-dollar homes are replaced by ramshackle cottages with boarded-up windows and screen doors without screens. There are no fancy automobiles, only drives filled with barely running beaters, skeletons of classics on blocks, and heaps of rusted-out parts. This is the poor South; this is the Tennessee I had been expecting.

I take my time through the backwoods slum, inspecting the jerry-rigged construction and do-it-yourself home repairs. I notice shingles piled beneath a roof's edge, blue plastic tarps taking their place. *Arff...arff... arff...* I hear the deep barks before I see the beasts. I pump my legs as hard as I can, shifting gears and riding high on the handlebars. *Arff...arff...arff...* Out of the corner of my eye I see a blackened streak, a wave of darkness on legs. It chases my rear wheel, lunging for rubber, stretching its neck, and longing for flesh. I push as hard as I can until the *arff...arff...arff...* begins to fade. When I finally feel that I am out of danger, I turn my head and see a half-dozen Rottweilers, as big as they can be, huffing and puffing, angry as all hell that their game has pulled away. *Arff...arff...arff...*

There must be a paved road coming along soon. It's been miles since I've seen any water to my left, and there haven't been any drastic turns on the path. But what the hell is that in front of me? I slow down. I stop my bike. Motherfucker! You've got to be fuckin' shittin' me! Fuckin' son-of-a-bitch cocksuckin' motherfucking' bullshit! How the fuck did this happen? Fuck...Fuck... Fuck...Fuck...

I breathe in. I breathe out. I breathe in. I breathe out. I work to regain my composure and assess the situation. On one hand, I've just ridden ten miles down a dirt road and have discovered where it goes. On the other hand, where it goes turns out to be a dead end. On the bright side, I finally understand why this road is not on the map. But unfortunately the bright side is merely a speck of light, barely blinking on this dark fuckin' day. I need to keep my composure. Oh shit, I've lost it. Fuck...Fuck... Fuck...Fuck...

There is nowhere to go except back from where I came. I turn around and head down the dirt road. This time I'm ready for the dogs. I give it all I've got, flying full speed ahead. By the time the beasts notice me, I am well past them. Though they do give chase, I leave them in the dust, only to hear their *arff…arff…arff…* trailing behind me. I pay little attention to the ramshackle cottages but am downright disgusted as I pass the country club. I now have a slight understanding of what it must feel like to be one of the poor souls who lives on the dirt road, forced to pass the green grasses of a capitalistic land grab every time they leave their homes.

Almost two hours after the fact, I am back where I started. With the sun creeping toward the horizon, I push hard, hoping to make up for lost time. Soon enough I am tired, so I stop at the remnants of a burned-out restaurant. I sneak around back to take a piss, hit a pipe, and calm my nerves. I peer through the cracked glass of a window and examine the devastation inside. The charred skeletal frame is coated with dark soot, the drywall gone, blackened two-by-fours climb out of the gray concrete floor, which is partially hidden beneath a paler shade of ash. There are no tables or chairs, no booths or stools—only the gutted remains.

With every hit of weed and every cloud of smoke that escapes my lungs, the more disturbing this place feels. In stillness I see movement: objects warping and contorting, and bending with vibration. In the quiet I hear noise: thuds, trickles, and laughter, plus ghosts of people who never died or never lived in the first place. A stream of paranoia creeps into my soul and forces me to question the nature of everything around me. The focus of my eyes fades backward, until I am no longer looking inside the ruin but at a person with long hair, stubble, green eyes, and pupils as big as the moon. I am afraid of this man until

I realize that it's my own reflection. I regret, I mean if I could go back, if I know what I know now, I never would have smoked that shit in the first place. And I don't know why, but I want to get out of here now!

I take off and the farther I get from the burnt-out building, the less paranoid I become, though an anchor of insecurity continues to weigh me down. The sun is fading fast, and I have to find somewhere to sleep. I hit a "T" in the road. A sign ahead points to Knoxville on the left and some place I've never heard of to the right. The last thing I want is to be caught in a large city after dark, so I take a right.

A few miles down I see a sign for a "Wilderness Area" so I swing a left and head up into the hills and shadows of early dusk. The road twists and turns into the backwoods until I finally arrive at my destination. I scout out the perimeter and decide that it's a safe place to spend the night. Then I remember that the only thing that I have eaten all day didn't stay in my body. My stomach is growling and my mouth feels as if it is filled with cotton balls. All my water bottles are empty, but I remember the sports drink I tucked into my saddlebags. I open the cover and find only an empty bottle. How could this be? It must have leaked out somehow. I inspect the gear that is tucked underneath. Nothing is so much as damp. I don't remember drinking it, but I must have, that's the only logical explanation.

Oh shit! Jon, you're going crazy. You're doing things without thinking, remembering things that didn't happen, and forgetting things that obviously did. You've been making decisions on instinct. You haven't looked at a map in hours. And not to mention, but to mention, you're talking to yourself in the third person again. Snap out of it! Bring yourself together! Wait, bring myself together. This was the hottest day that I have ever experienced in my life, temperatures over one hundred degrees Fahrenheit—the closest to hell that I've ever been. It's not the ganja that has fucked up my mind (though it probably hasn't helped), it's dehydration—sunstroke. I need water!

I head west, past a house that's set back in the trees. I know that I should just stop, knock on the door, and ask to fill my water bottles. But I can't bring myself to do it, too paranoid—visions of Southern stereotypes. I'm a "Yankee" in Tennessee. What if they don't accept my accent, my long hair, my beard, my bike? I pedal out of the forest, into the rolling hills of farmland, golden wheat as far as the eye can see. A "T" in the road; I take a left, then another, then a right, another, and another, until I have no idea where I am. And the sun is gone.

A car! I spot a car at a stop sign. I pump hard. At about 30 feet away, I realize it's a cop. A cop! Never in my life have I been so happy to run into law enforcement. Any other day and I would steer clear of the police. I hate them. But today I need their help. Protect and serve, that's what they're here for, to protect and serve. I am only 20 feet away when the cruiser rolls off in the opposite direction. I stop my bike, raise my arms in the air, wave my hands back and forth and yell, "Wait, stop, wait, I need your help, wait, stop, wait."

The car continues on its way. I reach to the ground, pick up a pile of loose gravel and toss it as far as I can. The small-scale meteor shower of grit lands across the cop's trunk and rear window, giving off the sudden clatter of hard rain. I immediately regret what I have just done.

The car comes to a sudden halt and then ever so slowly reverses until its bumper is just a couple feet in front of me. Expecting the worst, I walk my bike up to the driver's door. The window lowers to reveal a pot-bellied police officer with a chubby face and a bushy mustache. I wait for a scolding, a "What the fuck?" or "Are you out of your mind?" But instead he simply gives me a look of bewilderment and waits for me to speak.

"I'm sorry sir, but I seem to have gotten myself lost."

"Well luckily you got my attention, because to be perfectly honest, I didn't even see you there."

I am somewhat awestruck. *Luckily*?

"Where ya headed?"

"Just need to find a motel for the night."

"Oh jeez. Well, ain't gonna find nothin' out here. Gonna haf to go clear into Knoxville I reckon. Thas gonna be your best bet. And we're talkin' a good 15 miles."

"That's fine. If you could just point me in the right direction, I would be very grateful."

"Well let's see. Gonna go straight 'til this road ends, take a left and then your first right. Few miles down and there's a church. Take a right, no wait a second, a left, yes, a left at the church. Follow that 'til it ends, and then 'nother left and 'nother right and that road should take you clear into the city. From there, well, you're gonna haf to stop and ask where the closest motel is."

"All right, let's see if I got this. Straight until this road ends, a left, a right, another left at the church, one more left and then a right."

"Sounds about right."

"Thank you so much officer. Don't know what I would have done without you."

"Well, that's kinda what we're here for. Good luck."

The car pulls away and I follow behind, the gap between us getting larger by the second until I am on my own again. "Left, right, left, left, right," I sing the cadence out loud, over and over.

I follow the directions and am surprised to find them spot on. The fields gradually evolve to houses with green yards, churches, schools, and parking lots. But no stores, no food, and no water. By the time I pass a sign that reads Entering Knoxville City Limits, it is dark. Traffic has built up, and it's Friday night of Memorial Day weekend, and I know that people have been drinking. I have no lights on my bike, but there is only one thing on my mind—water.

Store! I hurry inside and beeline it toward the drink cooler. I grab a Gatorade and pour it down my throat. At this moment it is the single greatest thing that has ever touched my tongue. It's as if God herself squeezed heavenly nectar from between her loins and delivered it to Earth for this precise moment.

I grab two more bottles, an armful of snacks, and drop them next to the register. The guy behind the counter is short and fat with a receding hairline, goatee, and sideburns that hang down to the bottom of his jaw, his fat jaw. If I had to guess, I'd say that he most likely lives in his mother's basement and is obsessed with online role-playing games. I'd bet that in some alternate universe he has magical powers, secret potions, and a pet dragon. But in this universe I hope that he has good directions to the nearest motel.

"Motel, let's see," he says as he rings me up. "Gonna wanta go straight at the light, down a little hill, and you'll see a McDonald's. Swing a right. There's gonna be a whole shitload of stores and restaurants and what have you. Take a left where the Target used to be. Follow that for, I'd say, a good four or five miles. You'll come to a major road, lots of lights, lots of motels down that way."

"Where the Target used to be?"

"Yeah, gonna wanna take a left right before that."

"Thanks," I say as I head out the door. Where the Target used to be—how the hell am I supposed to know where the Target used to be? Fuck it, I'll stop somewhere and ask somebody else. Now that I'm finally thinking straight, I grab a flashlight, turn it on, and snug it under a bungee cord on my saddlebags. That way a drunk driver can see me before he hits me. I ride through the light, take a right at the McDonald's and hug the sidewalk as I pass a "shit-load of stores and restaurants." Just as I'm about to stop and ask for new directions I catch sight of *it*. At the top of a giant pole climbing maybe 40 feet in the air is a white sign with two faded red circles, one inside the other—bull's-eye—"where the Target used to be."

I take a left before the sign, follow a darkened road for four or five miles, holding my breath every time a car passes from behind. I come to a major road, lots of lights, motels as far as the eye can see. I find the shod-diest looking one and purchase a room from the Indian desk clerk. As I enter my room, a sense of relief fills my body. This horrible day is finally over. It's strange, even after dealing with a terrible hangover for the first half of the day, I could really go for a couple of beers. But I know I shouldn't, and so I don't. But I did notice a soda machine before I got to my room, and a cold refreshing soda sounds pretty damn good.

I walk out to the machine and am as happy as a man can be when I see that it carries Pepsi. I love Pepsi. It is by far my favorite liquid in the entire world. Don't get me wrong, there are other great colas out there, but for my money nothing compares to the sweet, crisp flavor of Pepsi. I remember a few years back, spending fourteen days in county jail, the first thing I did when I got released was buy a Pepsi; not a beer or a cigarette. A Pepsi. And now that I've seen the button on the machine, I have the same craving as I did that day. I slide a dollar bill into the slot, and it immediately spits it back out. I try a crisper bill and it does the same. Motherfucker! I hurry back to my room, rifle through my bags, and find exactly three quarters, the only three quarters that I have. Back outside, one at a time, they drop into the vending machine. I press the button that says Pepsi on it. Clunk, the aluminum can falls to the bottom. I reach down and grab it. What the fuck is this? A Diet Pepsi. There is nothing in the world that my taste buds hate more than the artificial sweetener used in diet sodas. Motherfucker! You've got to be shittin' me! Fuckin' son-of-a-bitch cocksuckin' motherfuckin' bullshit!

Back in the room I set the unopened Diet Pepsi on top of the television and turn it on. Exhausted, I remove my clothes and slide underneath the sheets. I stare at the screen and barely process the moving colors in front of me. A movie is playing, but I don't know what it is. I recognize Meryl Streep, but who's this other actress? Uh, Anne Hatha-what? Hathaway, that's it. What movie is this? Oh, I know, *The Devil Wears Prada*—the last movie on Earth that I would ever want to watch. I grab the remote off the nightstand and click the channel button. Nothing happens. I try the number buttons. Nothing. The power button. Nothing. I'm too tired to get up, so I leave it on and find myself somewhat enjoying it.

What a day, what a day. A bad day almost always starts with a hangover, but I know that never again, as long as I am alive, will it ever end with me in a fleabag motel in Knoxville, Tennessee, staring at *The Devil Wears Prada* and an unopened can of Diet Pepsi.

★

Jon Penfold lives in Portland, Oregon, where he's always looking for his next adventure. For more of his stories, please visit jonpenfold.com

The Holy Grail

Yoo-hoo, Dan Brown?

Standing in the doorway to the cathedral in Valencia, Spain, I couldn't help but think: Man, da Vinci didn't have a clue.

"*Está aquí?*"

"*Sí.*"

"*En la Catedral?*"

"*Sí.*"

"The Holy Grail?"

"Yes, señor."

The man taking tickets looked as though most of the salt in his salt-and-pepper hair was the result of people like me asking the same question three and four times. But in my defense, I had just unlocked one of the greatest secrets of the past two millennia pretty much by sheer dumb luck. I had succeeded where others had failed—Percival, the Knights Templar, Indiana Jones, Monty Python—and I wasn't even looking. All this talk about the chalice being a da Vinci-coded metaphor for Mary Magdalene, flushed away.

It turns out that the thirteenth-century Gothic cathedral, a blimp-hangar of a basilica built on the Plaza de la Reina in central Valencia, features some popular attractions for the tourists: a bell tower with a 207-step spiral staircase and an amazing citywide view; two paintings by Goya; the mummified arm of St. Vincent the Martyr; and, oh, by the way, a little trinket called the Holy Grail.

Yeah, *that* Holy Grail.

It seemed at the time as if that little fact was something the cruise director should have mentioned in the port briefing, even in passing: "Yes, folks, you'll find Valencia is a terrific, friendly port whose main attractions are the great shopping bargains and yummy Spanish paella, especially in the lovely plaza next to the church with that Holy Cup thingy."

Sure, cruise lines would rather not tell you everything about a port so you'll be more inclined to take the packaged excursion, but this seemed kind of extreme. It's a little like arriving at Skull Island and having the cruise staff tout the scenic, white-sand beaches and the colorful local culture, but neglect to mention the 20-story gorilla with a weakness for petite blondes.

It seemed, also, that the easiest job on the planet should be director of tourism for the city of Valencia. You arrive at the office, have a cup of coffee and then prepare for the toughest decision you'll make all day: should the next campaign emphasize the excellent climate, miles of beaches and historic district, or the fact that our city has exclusive display rights for the single most important relic and tangible icon of faith for, oh, say, a few billion Christians worldwide?

O.K., that's decided. Let's go to lunch and have yummy paella.

But I had already been to the tourist information office (not more than 100 yards from the cathedral), and no one made mention of grails, holy or otherwise. Maybe they were waiting for a leading question, such as, "Um, I don't suppose you folks have any enormously well-known and historically sought-after relics lying around?"

Similarly, in the guide put out by the Valencia Tourism & Convention Bureau, the first of only two references to the artifact isn't until Page 23, a 25-word description that doesn't get much more in-depth than that it was at the Last Supper. The second entry is even shorter, and both ranked in importance below El Tribunal de las Aguas (the Water Court), where local farmers settle irrigation disputes.

It turns out the Santo Caliz (Holy Chalice), a red agate cup with elaborate gold handles, was sent to Spain by Pope Sixtus II and soon-to-be-martyred St. Laurence when Rome was under siege in 258 A.D. According to one version of the story, it bounced around eastern Spain for a few hundred years, through the hands of monks and kings, until it was given to the church to hold—pawn-shop style—when Don Juan, King of Navarre, needed money to fund a small war. He never raised enough cash to get it out of hock, so the church has owned it since, moving it to the Cathedral of Valencia in 1437.

Apparently, nobody sent out a memo, so people have been looking for it for centuries.

I began to wonder what other mysterious missing relics are simply scattered around Spain. Is the Lost Ark of the Covenant really lost, or just buried under a stack of old hymnals in the cathedral at Barcelona?

Inside Valencia's cathedral, after admiring the Goyas and St. Vince's arm, I decided that before "discovering" the grail, I should prove myself worthy, Arthurian knight-style, by climbing the bell tower. At the top (207 steps and 30 overfed German tourists later), Valencia stretched in every direction, an unpretentious working city—probably the type of place where people wouldn't think to exploit a holy relic.

Had this thing made its way to, oh, say, Florida, the "cathedral" would likely be a glass and polished-steel monolith at the center of a sprawling theme park called Grail Land or Holywood. After a day of standing in line for the Water-to-Wine Log Ride and the KrazyKwest roller coaster (souvenir photos of riders are labeled "In Remembrance of Wheeee!"), the family would sit down for Chalice Cheeseburgers at the Last Supper Saloon.

Maybe it's best that it's kind of "lost" in Valencia.

As I descended the tower, questions swirled under my hat: Is it possible they're trying to keep it a secret? Is there a Valencia Code? Do I need Tom Hanks' mullet to break the code? Who dusts the Holy Grail?

Once back in the sanctuary, I found that the ticket guy was gone and the Chapel del Santo Caliz had closed for the day. No Holy Grail. My sacred quest, however brief, would have to wait for some other day.

I went back to see St. Vince's arm again and put five euros in the donation box—I thought it might go toward the effort to find the rest of the poor guy—and headed for the door.

Next quest: yummy paella.

★

Spud Hilton is the travel editor of the San Francisco Chronicle, *where since 2000 he has written about, reported on, and been hopelessly lost in destinations on six continents. His attempts to divine, describe, and defy the expectations of places—from*

Havana's back alleys to Kyoto's shrines to the floor of a hippie bus in Modesto—have earned ten Lowell Thomas Awards and have appeared in more than 60 newspapers in North America, several of which are still publishing. Spud also writes the Bad Latitude travel blog at SFGate.com and plays cornet in an early New Orleans traditional jazz band. A version of this story was previously published in the San Francisco Chronicle.

The Spittle Express

> *"Various other forms of behaviour perceived as
> antisocial in the West are considered perfectly normal in
> China. The widespread habit of spitting, for example,
> can be observed in buses, trains, restaurants and even
> inside people's homes. Outside the company of urban
> sophisticates, it would not occur to people that there was
> anything disrespectful in delivering a powerful spit while
> in conversation with a stranger."*
> —The Rough Guide to China

I'D READ THE WARNINGS. THE CHINESE LIKE TO SPIT. BUT after a year in Korea (spitting with the best of them), I assumed there wasn't much I hadn't seen when it comes to sputum. I was wrong. The average person in China sees spit as a multipurpose wonder formula: add to rice as a flavor enhancer; splatter on floors to keep the dust down; apply to neighbors' faces as a cleaning agent; apply to tables for the same reason; use on sliding windows and doors as a lubricant, plus it also stops sunbeams.

My first experiences with Chinese mucus were rather mild. I noticed that when the Chinese got together to stare at me, they'd blow their noses in my direction or would pick their noses and roll the boogers around in their fingers before offering me a handful of peanuts. They'd spit on my shoes or on their own shoes, or they'd spit on the floor and then would sit or lie down on top of it.

My aversion of flying phlegm increased when I was with my travel partner, Ted, on a bus trip to Hohhot. We sat in front of some serious country bumpkins, dressed in knit wool and fatigues. One of them had eyes as yellow as yolks. And he had a cold, or allergies. He kept grunting and blowing snot-jets from his nose onto my neck.

I'm pretty cantankerous and frank regarding certain issues, and I turned and glared at him. But he acted as if I wasn't even there. I received some spray from his nose right into my eyes. I made nasty upset-sounding noises (which didn't require translation) at him and wiped my face with my bandana, making sure he understood exactly how much I disliked the scenario. But it didn't work. He and his friends were getting a kick out of this.

Ted suggested they knew exactly how much I hated it, and to ignore them. I was sure they thought it was funny to see a white person, probably the only one they'd ever seen, acting uppity on a third-class bus. I didn't quit miming upset, and he didn't quit blowing his nose on my neck. At the next stop they left, and at Hohhot Ted took a train south while I took a train to Turpan and Urumqi.

The travel expert at the train station had told me these spots would be very hot this time of year. It was March, so I had my doubts. I'd lived in a high northern desert before. It was not hot there in March. But he insisted it was hot. I'd bought a ticket, wanting to see the Uighur, and wanting to ride a horse across wild country, and wanting to be able to tell people I'd been to one of the remotest spots on the planet.

It was not warm on the train ride. The wind blew constantly, rocking the drafty coal-fed train back and forth

on the tracks. Outside you could see dirt and snow flying
through the air in swirls. The ground was pitted like an old
minefield. The only people on the train were so hillbilly
they were possibly more scared of me than fascinated.

To add to the cold and grit, the floors, seats, and tables
were covered with slimy spat-out sunflower seed shells.
Nobody minded. Children were laid down on the floor,
where they played with the filthy piles. The children,
like everyone else, were dressed in knit-wool jumpsuits
but theirs had giant holes in the rear ends revealing their
bare butts. This would not have been so bad, except that
because of the lack of diapers the children were allowed to
shit anywhere. They shit in the aisles, on the tables, and on
the floors right next to the sunflower seed piles.

I was offended by this at first. Then I went to find a
toilet. The toilets were locked and porters guarded them,
shaking their heads when I motioned they should open
them. They kept refusing. I made a fuss but didn't get anywhere with it. So I made my way from car to car search-
ing for an open toilet. Finally, I found one that was not
guarded. Instead it was booby-trapped with turds smeared
all over the floor, walls, and the outer door. However, the
handle and lock were somewhat clean. The lock was not
actually a lock so much as an Allen-wrench hole. My knife
fit into it perfectly. I opened it and discovered why nobody
was allowed in the toilets. The floor was more than ankle
deep in shit. I found a relatively less filthy spot for my feet
outside the doorway, and unloaded into the room. After
that I did all of my business in Chinese trains by shit-
ting off the end of the caboose. And when it was warm
enough, a pack of children would chase along the tracks
after my bare caboose.

Sleeping in this kind of filth is exceptionally difficult.
There is nowhere to put down your head without getting

your ears wet. I managed to nap propping myself up by the hand. But my arm would inevitably fall asleep. I eventually managed to find a spot for myself because the further west we went the fewer people there were on the train. But now, those that did get on the train were frequently accompanied by gaggles of geese, a few goats, or some sheep. I didn't mind. Their shit stunk less. The conductor even allowed some pigs on the train—a rarity in the Muslim part of China. The hogs cleaned the floors almost sparkly, eating every turd in sight, and I was thankful for the few Buddhist swineherds allowed to ply their trade in these parts.

A skinny old man with a long beard sat with me, curiously eyeballing my big nose and green eyes. He was harmless, and he didn't spit so much. But then some cops boarded. They asked for his ticket. He didn't have one. They beat the shit out of him right in front of me. Two held his arms and a third kneed him in the groin. He cried out and went limp. Then the man in charge of the blows slammed down so hard with his elbow on the old man's shoulders that he lost consciousness. They rolled the old man out the door.

All of the cops then left except for one. This one sat across from me, chain smoking, spitting and gazing out the window into the dust storm. I wrapped myself up and lay down on the bench, closing my eyes and trying to forget what I just saw. But I couldn't. Because the cop kept spitting on me.

He had a peculiar way of spitting. He used his tongue, so that the spit would come out in a string that broke into a spray as it traveled through the air. In this way he managed to drench me. My shoulder, neck, ear, and face were all subjected to hours of spit.

Occasionally he would get up and I'd assume he was leaving for good. But he always came back, always with another cigarette and enough saliva to fill a swimming pool. I tried various means of showing him that I did not like it. I covered my face with my jacket. But it was too damn cold for that and after a couple minutes I was shivering.

I tried to demonstrate to him that I was disgusted. I grimaced, grunted, groaned, shook my head, wiped myself off, and stomped my wet feet. But he seemed oblivious, not even glancing at me to see what it was I tried to communicate. He didn't care. I was invisible.

Eventually I decided to be a little more blunt. I stood up, squared myself directly in front of him, and spat a big glob his way. I'd meant for it to land on the seat, right next to him. But I missed. It landed on his lap, in the vicinity of his crotch.

A tingle of apprehension shot through my limbs. I winced, prepared to receive a blow. I closed my eyes and scrunched up my face, hoping it would communicate to him how pathetic I was. I waited. Nothing. I peeked and saw that he hadn't changed position. He didn't even bother to look at me or wipe my glob from his groin. He just kept on staring out the window, dragging off his cigarette. Only now he had a slight smirk on his face, as if he were satisfied with something. Maybe he'd heard foreigners weren't as hip with spittle as the Chinese.

What could I do? I lay back down and closed my eyes. The cop remained across from me for another ten hours. But in that ten hours, never once did he spit, not even on the floor.

★

After a year in China and another in Turkey, Scott Morley is now in Vietnam journaling his family's expat experiences. He is a graduate of Antioch University, Los Angeles, with an M.F.A. in Creative Writing and is published in Larry Flynt's Big Brother Magazine, *Jeff Lebow's* Korea Bridge, *and Tom Glaister's* Tales of a Road Junky. *On Busan Web he published* The Mother-In-Law Diaries, *about raising his sons with his Korean mother-in-law. Scott has recently finished the novel* Hanson's Homeland, *about an American expat in Asia with a deep-seeded phobia of everything American.*

KATKA LAPELOSOVÁ

"'Allo! 'allo, 'allo, 'ahhhhhllo!"

Naked men in Budapest.

I'M IN BUDAPEST FOR THREE DAYS BY MYSELF. MY BOYFRIEND of two years and I broke up during a backpacking trip through Europe. After a discussion of mutually apathetic feelings culminating in, "I just don't love you anymore," Sean opted to cut his trip short and fly back to the United States. We had spent the weekend in Vienna, attempting to find locations from the film *Before Sunrise*. Slightly wounded, and looking for validation, I chose to forge ahead and explore the rest of our once-shared European itinerary—alone.

Can we all agree that "emotional schizophrenia" is one of the worst parts about breaking up with someone? Three hours sitting in an empty train car conjures up feelings of, "Oh my God, what was I *thinking*?!" followed by, "Why did we ever break up? I miss him…" and then, "Switzerland was amazing, the streets are practically made of chocolate!" and so on and so forth.

My real post-breakup issue is that I'm no good at striking up conversations with strangers. I find it to be awkward

and embarrassing and especially difficult when there is a
language barrier. Would my conflicting emotions prevent
me from enjoying this trip on my own?

It's surprisingly easy to enjoy my own company while
exploring Budapest during the day. No one thinks it's
weird to take photos at the Fisherman's Bastion or visit
the Museum of Fine Arts by myself. Even the Széchenyi
Bathhouse is welcoming to solo visitors. The Hungarian
language barrier turns out to be a blessing. It's nice to be
spared annoyingly probing questions like "Where is your
boyfriend?" or "Why aren't you married?"

But at night, everything changes. When the sun sets,
the world becomes suddenly intimate. Budapest's streets
are full of couples holding hands; laughter from groups of
friends echoes through the chilly air.

The excitement of hanging out with myself during
daylight fades, and I feel lonely. Where can an independent
woman hang out in the evening to avoid feeling awkward
and abandoned, where conversation and companionship is
not necessary for enjoyment?

The theatre, that's where.

A woman from my hostel gives me a brochure for *Un
Peu de Tendresse, Bordel de Merde!* (A Little Tenderness, For
Crying Out Loud!), a dance concert occurring in the
Józsefváros district of Budapest. The pamphlet displays a
pile of nude dancers lying on the floor.

I assume there will be nudity during the performance,
but this isn't a problem—as a fairly open-minded person,
naked people don't upset me. At the same time however,
I'd prefer not to be front-row-center, staring at a pair of
balls or a full-blown bush, three feet away from my face.
No, I'll take a seat somewhere in the middle.

Sitting in the middle means: "I'm O.K. with your naked
dancing—as long as I view it from a comfortable distance."

The Trafó House of Contemporary Arts is a revived warehouse-turned-theatre. This unique up-cycle of architecture is especially popular throughout many contemporary theatres of Eastern Europe. Seating is stadium style, so patrons look down at performers on a flat, ground-level stage.

Trafó is devoid of curtains and scenery; only the raw concrete and industrial piping of the original warehouse, with some stage lights hanging above it, are visible. In the center of the stage sits a man, on a chair—a naked man, with a full beard, wearing a long, blond wig.

He waves at the audience members as they file into the theatre. "'Allo!" he shrieks in a high-pitched voice. He sounds like a little girl. "'Allo! 'allo, 'allo, 'aaahhhh-hhllo!" I sit in my strategically selected seat in the middle of the crowd and watch as some other naked men sporadically join him. All of them sport full beards and long, blond wigs, and speak like children. They stand awkwardly together in a line at the front of the stage.

Seems like I made the right choice, I think, as I settle in comfortably. Any minute now, the show will start, and I'll have two hours of conversationless distraction. The first row of people certainly got what they paid for tonight, as none of the dancers are censored. The brochure wasn't kidding about this nudity thing.

A woman in a shiny black dress closes the theatre's door and walks across the stage. The crowd reacts by hushing their pre-performance chatter. The woman is reminiscent of a modern-day Morticia from the *Addams Family*: inky-black hair and creamy skin, enhanced with bright red lipstick.

She explains that, due to the international nature of the theatre festival, the show will be performed in English, by a French-Canadian dance troupe, with Hungarian subtitles displayed on the back wall of the warehouse. The naked men behind her fidget and giggle every so often.

"Yes, there will be nudity," the woman, who introduces herself as the emcee, says to us. "But we're all adults, are we not? Surely, these performers don't intimidate anyone here."

At this, the bizarrely cross-dressed males begin to dance. Pelvises are thrust into the faces of those sitting in the front row. Bare buttocks are pressed onto the laps of unsuspecting audience members. The fourth wall has been broken, the dancers have infiltrated the sacred ground of the viewers. The rest of the audience can't help but laugh at the victims in the first row, who probably didn't think they'd get harassed when innocently choosing their seats.

"Oh!" the emcee shouts at us. "You think it's funny? You think you people in the back of the theatre are safe and sound? Well, think again!"

The dancers tear through the audience, leaving no chair inviolate. They run up and down the aisles, skip through every row, and clumsily climb over people. The men are like a pack of clownish-looking lions, and we are all their vulnerable prey. Absolutely no one is safe. Those affected by this act of insanity include old women, young men, lovey-dovey couples, and one especially hysterical American female who absolutely cannot stop laughing.

Tears stream down my face. I'm laughing so hard it's almost difficult to breathe, an asphyxiating kind of enjoyment that brings mild pain from pleasure. I am doubled over in my seat, my body retching with delight from this unexpected turn of events.

And then, I'm spotted. Who else but the original naked man, who greeted the audience with his bizarre, high-pitched salutation "'Allo!" only 15 minutes before, should single me out from the rest?

His face becomes long in a frown as he climbs over the two rows of people in front of me, his buttocks dangerously close to a bald man's face, his genitalia hanging loose above another woman's perm. Standing before me, he looks concerned.

"Oh no!" he whimpers girlishly. "Oh no, why are you crying! Don't cry! Why are you sad?!"

I can't answer him; pockets of air from silent laughter choke back any words I can possibly respond with.

"I'll be your boyfriend!" he suggests. Oh sure, that's just what I need now, another crazy boyfriend. As though it were no odd question, he has the audacity to ask, "Do you want to touch my penis?"

Oh my god.

"Look!" he beckons, thinking I need further convincing. "Look, it does tricks!"

Dancing Naked Man #1 gyrates his hips like he's wearing an invisible hula-hoop. His flaccid penis begins swirling in the air, like a pinwheel spinning rapidly in the wind.

I've lost all control of emotion. Any post-traumatic-breakup feelings I may have felt prior to attending this show have completely dissolved. I didn't think men were capable of such feats. It's certainly a talent Sean didn't possess. Maybe I should give this guy a shot; who knows what kind of kinky stuff he's into?

This display of nude acrobatics continues for a moment as I attempt to steady myself on my chair. Falling off my seat from laughter could mean "getting to third base" quicker than I anticipated.

Despite this inception of comfort, no one leaves the arena. Maybe it's because Europeans have different perceptions of personal space than where I come from. I like to think, however, that the reason we all stay is the fact that, as the emcee alluded to, no one was safe. We all experienced a false sense of security, and we all came out of it unscathed. Something unexpected occurred, but no one got hurt— what else did we need to worry about? This is going to be a bizarre performance, but we're all in this together. This is an evening we'll never forget.

The emcee calls the dancers back to the stage to formally begin the show. My breathing slows, I wipe rivers of tears away from my cheeks, sniffle snot back into my nose and attempt to compose myself once more.

The show begins, and I'm enchanted by what becomes one of the most beautiful, emotionally responsive evenings of my life. The dancers, both clothed and nude, delight me, anger me, make me feel loved and even lonelier. The important result is that *Un Peu de Tendresse, Bordel de Merde!* made me *feel*.

I walked into the Trafó House of Contemporary Arts as a socially awkward, recently dumped young woman. At the end of the performance, I walk out of the theatre knowing that no one back home will ever understand what happened to me tonight.

But I'll understand it, I'll remember it. I'll recognize how I sat in that theatre, watching a naked man wave hello to me from the middle of a bare stage, thinking to myself that I'd be safe and that this performance was "safe" and that life, in general, was "safe." That being in a relationship was "safe" merely because it provided me with someone to talk to in the evenings.

Since that intoxicating night in Budapest, I've travelled to over fifteen countries on my own. I've learned to relax, to open myself up and trust others, to recognize that there are times when I can be happy on my own and times when companionship is necessary, and needed.

When the latter arises, I build up the courage to talk to strangers and see where things go. I've met best friends, boyfriends, old friends and insane friends, simply by asking them this: "What's the craziest thing that's ever happened to you?"

You know my story. It started with "'Allo!" and ended with a bit of unsolicited genitalia, swinging six inches from my face.

★

Katka Lapelosová is a Managing Editor and the Director of Social Media at Matador Network. She is based in New York and likes speaking Czech when she's had one too many Pilsners. Her first eBook, 101 Guys to Date Before You Die, *launched in 2013. Other publications include articles for* Reader's Digest, GM's Drive the District, Thought Catalog, Travel Fashion Girl, Yelp!, Groupon, *and eight entries in the recently published* 101 Places to Get F★cked Up Before You Die. *Follow her on* Twitter *at @KatkaTravels for 140-characters worth of travel antics.*

KEPH SENETT

A Bed of Fists

Putin's queerly obsessed.

BEFORE I'D LEFT FOR RUSSIA—BEFORE I'D EVEN BOOKED MY tickets on Aeroflot, the airline with the world's least buoyant name—my father and I tossed around the exact nature of a Soviet-era sofa bed.

"It won't be built for comfort," he said, to which I replied, "Nor, I hope, for speed."

I considered the matter then offered, "It will have no springs, maybe, because springs are ostentatious."

"Or," he responded darkly, "it will be *all* springs."

Only ten minutes on Russian soil, and I was convinced my dad had been right about "all springs." The airport was predictably dreary, and dodgy airport nachos or nerves had left me flatulent and nauseated. I found the kiosk selling shuttle tickets, but the agent didn't look up from her newspaper, preferring instead to tap the back of her manicured fingernail against the window that separated us. I followed her gesture to a brochure taped to the glass. Presumably, it contained ticket prices and a timetable, but it was no more use to me than the agent—it was written in Cyrillic.

"Do you have anything in English?" I asked. Without looking up, she shook her head. This agent was definitely giving me *all the springs.* A cramp ripped through my abdomen, and I went to find a toilet.

Mercifully, the bathroom signs at Sheremetyevo were completely familiar. I picked out the lady in her triangle skirt from 50 yards away and scooted toward her without unclenching my ass cheeks. I pushed open the door, but instead of a row of stalls I was faced with another woman behind glass. Eyes wide—she shouted and waved her hands. I fumbled in my jeans to retrieve rubles but no matter how many bills I shoved under the screen, she kept yelling and gesturing. Finally, she let herself out of the booth, grabbed me by the arm and pulled me back into the hall. With no break in her tirade, she dragged me around the corner and pointed toward another door marked by a stick figure in pants. I jerked my arm loose, unzipped my jacket, and pointed indignantly at my breasts. Without breaking stride, the woman shrugged and tugged at her hair as if to say, "Well what do you expect looking like that?"

I arrived on Konstantin's doorstep unsure if I'd shit my pants. The answer—thankfully—was no, but upon being presented with a welcome fish caught fresh from the river, I vomited into my teacup. The activists in Konstantin's tiny kitchen were either being polite or didn't notice, having just received the alarming news that the authorities had threatened our host hotel management until they withdrew our reservation. Without a venue, there would be no human rights conference. As the activists smoked and shouted at each other under the buzzing fluorescent, I crept into the bedroom looking for refuge.

The sofa bed was open—an unfurled blini. A large photograph on the wall commemorated a sports event the Russian LGBT Sports Federation had put on the previous year. Local athletes had gathered outside Moscow to ski and snowboard in the anonymity of an unmarked stretch of forest. Smiling activists holding rainbow flags surrounded Konstantin, who wore a prim, close-lipped smile. His hands hung loosely at his sides, and his collar, as always, was buttoned right to his throat.

I lowered myself onto the bed. It was far scratchier than necessary. Macho growls erupted from the kitchen, breathy fricatives of Russian spoken under duress. I pulled the blanket over my legs. Not quite comfortable, I shifted, rolled, and shifted again. I closed my eyes and tried to ignore the knobs of stuffing jabbing my ribs. There were a thousand reasons why my paperwork should have been denied—I'm a writer and an LGBT activist, for starters—but despite a comprehensive application form ("Do you have any specialized skills, training or experience related to firearms and explosives, or to nuclear matters, biological or chemical substance?"), somehow I'd been granted my visa. From the comfort of my apartment in Toronto, flying into Putin's Russia on a tourist visa with a fake hotel reservation and my soccer gear hadn't seemed utterly daft. Now, I wasn't so sure. I rolled onto my back and stared into the dark. Cigarette smoke drifted in from the next room. My bowels rumbled. I made a mental note to tell my dad: a Soviet-era fold-out couch feels like a bed of fists.

During the intensity of the 2014 Sochi Olympic Games, my friends in Canada, the United States, and around the world had signed petitions and poured vodka into the gutters to protest the anti-gay sentiment coming from Putin's administration. From inside the country, dissenters were much more circumspect. I could see why. Putin was brimming with contempt, and he'd proven to be extravagantly punitive. When Pussy Riot donned brightly colored balaclavas and sang a protest song on the steps of a Moscow cathedral, he'd stripped to the waist and threw the women in jail for two years of hard labor. I really didn't want to be sent to a Russian work camp.

"'Oh, gays,' they say. 'They are going to nightclubs and they wear pink pants.'" I was standing in a freezing parking lot taking instruction from Elvina, cofounder of the Russian LGBT Sports Federation, who was briefing me on how "the homophobes" (as she called them) perceive gay people in Russia. I flashed-back on '70s images: a thin, fey man—with a purse draped over an arm, perhaps—in tight pants and a floral blouse, wrist as limp as if broken. These were the faggots Putin feared and hated so much, so this was where we had to begin. In an effort to replace that caricature with a brawnier, sportier representation—one that fit more easily into a world ruled by a shirtless bully on horseback—the Federation had organized their Open Games and asked international activists to show up.

My father had been amused when I told him I was going to play soccer in Russia, in February. "Let me get this straight," he'd said. "You've decided to winter in…Siberia?" At the time, I'd chuckled along with him—nobody is more entertained by my folly than I—but now that I was waiting for the police to complete a bomb sweep on the venue for our opening ceremonies, it was all somewhat less hilarious.

"Give me your phone," Elvina ordered, releasing a plume of cigarette smoke. "Mine's blocked."

I handed her the ancient Nokia loaner I was carrying. She dialed, jabbing angrily, and began shouting into the mouthpiece in Russian, drawing the attention of all assembled. Dressed in black from her high-heeled boots to her turtleneck and wrapped tightly in a short trench coat cinched snugly around her waist, Elvina possessed the air of an operative. I zipped my lumpy down jacket to the chin and looked around the lot. Just outside the entrance, clusters of police stood beside their cars, stamping their feet and peering at our group through the gates. We numbered in the low dozens. I knew from Elvina that I was the only Canadian but that there were also German, Swedish, and French activists joining the Russians. Although some people huddled around the heaters in their cars, most had chosen to wait out the sweep indoors. Of those of us in the lot, everyone was white, and everyone was an adult. The country's anti-gay propaganda law—which made being out as LGBT an offense against minors—had forced the organizers to exclude anyone under 18 years old.

Elvina dropped her cigarette and handed back the Nokia. "Are you hungry?" To my surprise, she led me directly into a café in the basement of the same building we'd been waiting to have cleared of explosives.

"Shouldn't we go somewhere else?" I asked.

"There's no problem. The homophobes have found a new way to cancel LGBT events. An anonymous call to police about a bomb and the police must react."

"But how did they even know we'd be here?" The location had been kept secret even from participants until earlier that day.

"A leak," Elvina said. "Welcome to Russia."

A server scuttled over with menus and hovered while Elvina ordered for us. At the bar, several waiters in vests and dress pants convened, glancing toward the entrance. The other booths were filled with young people—members of our group—in ski jackets and knit caps warming their hands over steaming pots of tea, and old men in shiny suits spooning back soup without taking their eyes off us. Frantic disco played softly from two enormous speakers flanking a tiny, incongruent dance floor.

Our waiter returned with a tray holding two cups, a teapot, and a bowl of soup that he placed rather deliberately on the table. He said something to Elvina in Russian that made her shout at him. He shouted back and produced a credit card terminal. I reached for my cash but Elvina waved me away. She paid and the waiter left.

"What *was* that?" I asked, "Should we go?"

"No, sit. They just wanted us to pay now in case we are taken by police."

I considered the soup in its dainty ceramic bowl. There was a fussy pattern around the lip that matched the accompanying crouton urn. I tried to dress my meal using the souvenir-sized serving spoon, but after failing to ferry even a single morsel, I upended the entire pot into my bowl. The soup was unchallenging—mushroom. I guessed that Elvina had seen me defile Konstantin's teacup after all. While I ate, Elvina smoked and watched the door.

By the time the police dogs led a cadre of officials into the café, I'd finished. The handsome shepherds were alert, held close by cops in jackets marked in Cyrillic. Everyone except the shiny suited men rose and filed up the stairs.

The sun was down, and the parking lot damp. Everyone was looking to Elvina for answers, and I trailed her impotently as she paced and parried, fielding an urgent stream of questions. Unable to understand the language, much less the content of the conversation, I simply occupied the space to her left, the top of my head level with her armpit. Then, abruptly, she strode out of the parking lot, a pack of people in her footsteps. They were down the block before I realized I'd been left behind, so I took off after them, calling out Elvina's name. When I reached her, we stuttered at each other, her embarrassment at forgetting me competing with my discomfort with my own helplessness.

"O.K.," she said. "The organizers have to talk. Everyone will wait for us at McDonald's. Go with Roman." She pointed at a slouching man, and when I raised my eyebrows, she added, "He's a cameraman, for German television." Everything about Roman, from his posture to his floppy bangs, was easy and relaxed, but I was queer in Moscow, and it was dark, and there was a bomb, maybe. Before I could respond, Elvina was a block away, a smudge animated by puffs of cigarette smoke.

Roman made friendly small talk while we drove, headlights steady and fluid against the demented strobe of Moscow traffic. Outside the McDonald's, Roman looked for a space. Through the super-sized picture windows under the golden arches I could see that the place—a two-story behemoth with an interior balcony—was packed. Inside, a crowd of hungry people crushed against the counters, and the pong of hot salt and grease on packing paper with just the suggestion of meat permeated my clothes. Big Macs and Filet o' Fishes smell the same everywhere. Upstairs, all the seats were occupied. People had sussed out spots on the floor and plugged their phones in; some folks had laptops open, and the clacking of keystrokes added to the din. The line to the bathroom ran out into the hall. I exchanged shy smiles with several people whose faces I recognized from the parking lot, and by the time I returned to Roman's side I felt like I was in friendly territory.

Roman's English was impeccable, and he was easy to talk to. He was the first Russian I'd spoken to about the political situation for LGBT people who was neither an activist nor a homophobe.

It was close to midnight when the call finally came, and the dispatch was kept as short as possible. Someone took the message—nothing more incendiary than the name of a nightclub—and passed it on, lips to ear. In this immediate and untraceable way, our next location was passed from person to person and en masse we left.

Elvina was beside me suddenly. "You are good?" she asked. I nodded. "Good, I will see you there." Roman and I were back in the car with him trying to negotiate the parking lot, when Elvina knocked on my window. "Do you have room for one more?" She opened the door, a woman got in, and we were off. In the rearview mirror, friendly eyes smiled. I introduced myself; she said her name was Katya.

Roman knew the nightclub and got us there quickly. It looked completely ordinary: glass doors opened to a foyer with a staircase that delivered us into a subterranean pub. It was loud and smoky and the liveliest place I'd seen on my short visit to the city. Roman disappeared into the crowd, and Katya and I joined Elvina at the packed bar, where we flapped our rubles at the bartenders.

"O.K., we have the space in the back!" Elvina shouted over the rock music. Her cheeks were ruddy. She pointed to a set of drapes at the foot of the stairs, guarded by a serious-looking guy in a serious-looking suit. I left my rubles and an order for a glass of red with Katya and approached the door. Before I could bother the curtains, the man shot out an arm.

"Nobody goes in here."

"I'm with the Open Games," I assured him. "I just want to check out the space."

"There is nothing in here," he said.

"*We* are in here," I said, smiling. "I just want to see the space."

"There is nothing in here."

Just then I noticed Konstantin coming down the stairs and opened my arms for a hug. He placed a chaste kiss on my cheek. I shot a look at the doorman, but he was obstinately staring into the empty space above me.

"How are you doing?" I asked. Konstantin looked exhausted.

"I am O.K...there have been more cancellations." Since the bomb threat, the host venues for badminton, swimming, volleyball, and tennis had withdrawn our reservations. "They cancelled the athletes' host hotel," he said, his eyes red-rimmed. "They said we could not stay because there are children there." He forced a smile and walked through the curtains.

I returned to the bar and slid in next to Katya, who had the triumphant look of someone who's finally procured drinks. In her leather sports jacket and Clark Kent glasses, I thought she looked like Jodie Foster, if she were cast in the role of Nancy Drew. I wasn't that far off. Katya was a fellow writer—a reporter.

"I got you a drink," she chuckled, and offered me an absurdly small glass. "It looks like they're worried about you."

It was after midnight when, for the second time that evening, a message passed person to person through the crowd. They were ready for us in the back.

The room under the stairs was long and dim and filling with people. As Katya and I found space at a table with the German football team, Elvina and Konstantin mounted a low stage. The club owners didn't want the other patrons to know we were there, Elvina said, so we were asked to make no noise. She waved her hands above her head, modeling the silent gesture we were asked to use in place of applause. The crowd waved back furiously.

It was approaching three o'clock by the time the ceremony ended. My throat was sore from the cigarette smoke, and it was way past my bedtime. Elvina helped me find a ride home—not to Konstanin's this time but to Natalia's, another friend who had more space. Neither she nor Konstantin joined me; their night wasn't over. They had to find alternate venues before the Games began in the morning.

I woke up late the next day, stirred by the frustrated mewling of Frankie the cat, who was perambulating around the room trying to relieve her heat. I stretched out on the firm, modern sofa bed and prepared to rise. The clacking of nails on a keyboard along with the bitter smell of old coffee drew me into the kitchen, where Elvina and Natalia were huddled over a laptop.

"More cancellations, more police," Elvina said.

"Good morning," I replied, and poured a cup of coffee. *Are you fucking kidding me?* Though I'd been in Moscow for only a few days, I was already frustrated by the chaos.

Elvina's phone rang, and she left the kitchen, shouting in Russian.

"Are any of the sports happening today?" I asked Natalia.

"It depends. We're working on it. There's still the party tonight, at Ustritsa," Natalia said, with a shy smile. "It means 'oyster,' the bar. It's for lesbians."

Elvina strode back into the kitchen. "The police showed up and pulled everyone off the rink at Konstantin's skating workshop. They said there was a 'technical problem' with the ice." She rolled her eyes and sat at the laptop. I decided to go out and see Moscow.

Even though this trip wasn't exactly a vacation, once on the streets I felt the tug of adventure. At Belorusskaya, I pulled open the station doors and fished out the fare card Natalia had loaned me. I fed it into a likely looking slot and waited. The machine responded in Cyrillic.

On the one hand, there are the Romance languages. French, Spanish, and Portuguese do a fine job of confounding with their inverse sentence structures and their dizzying selection of tenses. Languages based on different alphabets like Arabic or Tamil, or—even worse—on logo-grams like Japanese belong to a class I call "Oh, just forget it." But Cyrillic makes you feel dim. Scattered in with the unfamiliar shapes there are enough recognizable letters that you think you could read it, if only you tried a lit-tle harder. I stood and squinted. After several moments of trying a little harder, I pushed a fistful of rubles into the coin drop and was gratified to see a tally adding up on the screen. I let myself in through the turnstiles, head held high.

Inside, throngs of people jostled and pressed, a miser-able mass moving toward the escalator, where the clot divided and reformed as a single line of people stand-ing right, one Russian to a stair. I jockeyed and found a place. It took three minutes to reach the bottom, long enough to wonder at the contrast between the frowning commuters and the backlit posters advertising holidays in places by azure waters. It was also long enough for me to get a gander at a woman who surely has one of the most wretched jobs in all of Moscow. In her severe blue uniform and forage cap, the woman shared a glass box no bigger than a telephone booth with a bank of secu-rity monitors and a microphone. The mic was for when someone would break the escalator rules—by standing left, for example. The windows were so she could dole out her imperious stink-eye.

Souvenir shopping in Moscow was a slog. I had just abandoned sifting through the heaps of *matryoshka* nest-ing dolls and Lenin shit when I saw it. I brought the Putin fridge magnet to the cash register and called it a day. I grabbed dinner at a Japanese restaurant. Ordering sushi off a menu in Cyrillic takes about as long as you'd expect, and I got back to Natalia's late. The apartment was empty. I sent texts to every number programmed into my Nokia.

"We are at Ustritsa near Mendeleevskaya," Katya replied. "Come now. I will get you at the Metro."

"Do you have a number for a taxi?" I wrote.

"Take the Metro. It's safer."

Natalia's neighborhood looked different at night. Storefronts and cafés that had overflowed with music and patrons only a few hours earlier were dark and quiet. Occasional headlights upset long shadows, and I frightened a cat feasting from a garbage bin. I was jumpy—and guilty. Amid all the joking between my father and me, he'd extracted a single solemn swear: "Promise me you won't walk around Moscow alone after dark." In his face I could see his sincerest worry and pride and respect. Without hesitation, I'd agreed. Now, with a hammering heart, I hurried toward the Metro.

I yanked open the station doors for the second time that day and stood in the shelter of the tiny foyer, pausing to catch my breath. I noticed someone to my left. A man in rags the color of dust with a mess of hair had jammed his arm into an ornate vent on the far wall. He was suspended, his weight borne by that tender fulcrum in the armpit. His eyes were closed and he hung still, but I knew he wasn't dead. No one would be allowed to sleep on the street in Moscow, I realized. This dusty man in Belorusskaya station had discovered an ingenious way to keep warm.

Ustritsa was on a narrow street hidden somewhere behind the Metro. I was glad for Katya's company, but I wondered why a taxi wouldn't have been better. "There aren't really taxis in Moscow," she said, then allowed that there are taxi companies but no reason to use them. Muscovites needing a ride flag cars on the street and negotiate a price with whoever pulls over. And the drivers? "Immigrants, those who can't get work, those wanting to make some extra money," she said. "It's not safe if you don't speak Russian." I wondered if it was safe if you do.

"Hey, I heard you went out for an adventure today," Katya said.

"I went shopping. I bought a Putin magnet. It's one of those that changes depending on how you look at it. From the left, it's young Putin, and as you turn it he gets old. He's got the same sour look, though, the whole way through. Which reminds me, what's the deal with Russians not smiling?"

"Yes, there is even a saying in Russian! It's that if you smile without a reason, you're an idiot." Katya, who I learned was Latvian, beamed at me.

The entrance to the club was unmarked except for two pale men in suits framing the doorway like potted plants. Once past security, we were plunged into darkness. "It's upstairs," Katya said. "Watch your step." I climbed with my hands thrust out in front of me, the faint thump of dance music and reek of cigarette smoke intensifying on each landing. At the top, strobe lights spilled into the hall. A poster on the wall used both Russian and an illustration to get its message across: no photographs.

Inside, the place was packed. People shouted over the dance music and clinking glasses. After a while, the DJ turned the music down, and Elvina took the stage. She announced that the skating, volleyball, and badminton had all been shut down by the police. The crowd booed. However, she continued, the table tennis competition went unmolested. The crowd cheered. At her invitation, the participants came to the stage and bent to accept their medals. Cast in shades of gold, silver, and bronze, each award was a square piece of glass the size of a drink coaster, decorated by a local artist. The words "Russian Open Games" were etched into the back so faintly that they were almost invisible. A person—a police officer, for example, or an airport official—would have to turn them just so to make out what was engraved there. Everybody applauded, the music was turned up, and a couple hundred LGBT people from Russia and beyond drank and danced the night away in a secret club on the third floor of a building on a back street in Moscow.

And so it went in the coming days. We would doggedly rise, gather our equipment, and trek to a location circulated last minute by text. Then we would play for fifteen minutes, or five, or not at all because the police would already be there, waiting. In the evenings, we'd reconvene to commiserate and exchange information. During the nights the organizers worked their contacts, looking for new locations that might allow us in.

By the fourth day of the Games, not a single event had been spared a visit by the authorities. When the basketball tournament was interrupted by a smoke bomb hurled onto the court during a match, judging by the speed at which the police showed up, many felt it likely that they'd been behind the attack. That evening, realizing that they'd lost control of the situation, Konstantin and Elvina told us that they could no longer guarantee our safety. If any of us wanted to leave, they said, they would understand. No one fled, but every one of us knew that we were no longer there for the sport.

I was registered to compete in the indoor soccer tournament. I'd signed onto Team Paris along with French activists I'd met the previous summer. It was a bright morning the day of our competition—clear and filled with birdsong. At the venue, Elvina was in a huddle with the other organizers, so my team and I hung back. Where the sun broke through the tangles of bare tree branches, it warmed our skin. As we waited, other soccer players began to emerge from behind parked cars. "Has anyone seen police?" someone asked. None of us had, and none of us could believe it.

Suddenly, Elvina broke away from her group. "Hurry!" she urged. "Let's get started!"

Inside, we dashed into the change rooms and hastily stripped down, shedding parkas and boots and jeans to pull on shorts and tennis shoes.

"Is there a bathroom in here?" someone asked. "Yes, but no toilet paper," came the reply. A third person called out, "Front pocket!" offering the private stash from her gym bag.

Out on the court, soccer players warmed up by volleying balls off the walls, firing shots at their goalies, and running wind sprints up and down the sides of the gym. Every time the rubber made contact with cement or the floor or flesh, it produced a familiar and satisfying crack. The space filled with shouting and sweat. I watched from the door, but only for a minute before I leapt out into the fray to play with my friends.

Someone had a camera on a tripod. Behind the goalie crease, they were filming a group of people in formal dress. When I approached, Elvina introduced me, a mischievous look on her face. "This is Edith Schippers, the Dutch Minister of Health and Sport. The police won't visit while she's here." I thanked the Minister, shook her hand, and bounded back onto the pitch.

Minister Schippers stayed as long as she could—long enough for two matches to play out—but her duties demanded she be elsewhere. The door to the gym had barely shut behind her before it was flung open again. Burly men in plain clothes followed by uniformed cops flooded in, shouting. Several of the Russian-speakers including Elvina advanced on them, shouting back. Katya held her press identification in front of her like a shield and demanded answers. Several people had pulled out cameras and phones and were recording the altercation. I got close enough to show solidarity, but no closer.

"O.K., come outside everybody," Elvina said, and everybody groaned. People complained in Swedish and English and French. Cold and grumbling, we filed out into the parking lot. Those with cameras documented the incident, pointing their lenses at the police and the vans in the yard. Some of us gave interviews. The police stood by, studying our faces.

"I'm going back to the Bureau. I'll text you later," Katya said. While she was at her desk writing the report—one of the few to appear in the Moscow press during the Games—we walked to a nearby McDonald's to take advantage of their wi-fi and warmth. It was more than an hour before the police declared the gym "safe" and allowed us to return.

After a few improvised changes to the schedule, the tournament resumed, but I was exhausted from standing around in the cold in my soccer shorts. Unable to match the stamina of my younger teammates, I watched from the sidelines.

My Games were over, but the truth was, I'd seen enough of Moscow.

Keph Senett is a Canadian writer and activist whose passions for travel and soccer have led her to play the beautiful game on four continents. She writes about human rights, LGBT and gender, soccer, and her own folly. Keph spends her free time trying to figure out how to qualify for a soccer squad in Asia, Australia, or Antarctica.

DAWN MATHESON

The Big Forehead of Newfoundland

Screech!

THERE ARE SO MANY DEVILISH LITTLE THOUGHTS THAT PERsist in our minds, aren't there? Most anyone I've known who said they don't have dirty thoughts—never fantasized their coworker naked, never pictured pushing their neighbor off the roof, or imagined crushing a frog with their foot—have ended up acting on these things. That's a far more dangerous mind.

My one friend who said she would never think a sexual thought about another man while married was the first to have a raunchy affair. Me, I can't stop these thoughts and I'm glad; they keep me, my coworkers, frogs everywhere, safe.

They say that traveling with someone can seal or end a relationship—at the very least, make strangers intimate, desired or not.

Take this example. I once went traveling with a man I'd just met on a yoga ashram in the States to his small cove town in Newfoundland. I certainly didn't fantasize an affair with "Gerard"; we were *seva* (selfless service) buddies, having bonded while cleaning toilets as part of a *spiritual cleanse*. This guy was doing his masters in Jungian psychology, which intrigued me. Plus, who says "no" to travel with strangers? It's usually far more successful than holidaying with one's family. It's about the expectations. Plus, we all know that the best way to see a place is from the inside, staying in the homes of those who live there.

Within 15 minutes of my arrival, Gerard began to drive me mad—that nasal voice advising me through thin lips that I had father issues. His insisting that my dreams of the previous night were cause for my morning moods. And that quiet request he made to his childhood friends to be called Gerard instead of Ger-bear.

All that superciliousness (well, that's how I saw it) came from a shiny bulbous forehead I hadn't noticed during early morning yoga on the ashram. Now it was all I could see.

Naturally, I imagined an ice pick cracking it open. Pop! That arrogance released like a green cloud into the salty Atlantic. Carefully placed dead center where the skull bones meet, a light tap on the handle and CRACK! What immense relief it provided, and, hey, no harm done.

I filled my days with this perfect image while taking photos at Signal Hill, bird watching at shore, stepping over fish guts down at the dock. It made for a very tolerable week's vacation.

With his big head out of the way, I was able to notice that Newfoundlanders do indeed eat a lot of fish, drink lots, and say words funny like "hoik" for hike (which I was forever out on in order to be alone with my ice-pick revery). The wind really is so strong that you can safely lean at a 45-degree angle into a strong gust when standing at sea on a cliff edge—making it very difficult to push someone off. Most men on The Rock marry by twenty and nearly all sport a moustache, or so it seemed. Red-cheeked neighbors do sit at kitchen tables in unlocked homes, laugh and drink whiskey over lunch.

Our hostess, Gerard's aunt, the only one in the house still employed, worked at the Sears catalogue outlet store. She smoked upon rising, served black coffee with squinting, smiling eyes, fluffed the best pillow in the house just for me, and whipped up variations of fish three times a day during my four-day visit. I was given no end of gifts, in spite of the family's minimal income: a large ceramic lobster, a mini-wicker lighthouse, even a locket. Inside was a picture of this near-stranger lady and her husband. Lovers have never thought to give me such an intimate gift.

Thank God it was in Newfoundland where all those airplanes were grounded on September 11. More than 6,000 people were promptly screeched-in, destined to down whiskey and kiss cod at kitchen tables until the airspace reopened.

With such kindness, I had twinges of guilt over my head-cracking fantasies of their Newfie nephew. I had tried to convince myself that I was being generous, thinking the thoughts on behalf of the whole fishing community. Taking the hit for the team. What the aunts and uncles must have thought of their large-headed boy, the picture he carried around of his guru, his arrogant moustache-less goatee! He didn't even drink whiskey; he toted his own chai.

Gerry hadn't just "gone away," he went "way away."

My fantasy reigned supreme until the very last moment, when it was smashed to smithereens. At the airport in St. John's, the kind auntie and leathery uncle couldn't stop the tears. They begged Ger-bear to write, phone home, and return soon. How they loved their boy!

Then the aunt did the unthinkable. She kissed Gerard on the forehead.

★

Dawn Matheson is a traveler, writer, and multimedia story pro-ducer from Guelph, Canada. She's told audio stories on CBC Radio, video stories on gallery walls and in outdoor installations across Canada, plus written travel tales for numerous national publications. Find her ramblings at thiswasnow.com

SARAH ENELOW

A Real Piece of Americana

What's black-black?

I STOOD ALONE AT THE BAR AT DOUG & MARTY'S, A SMALL expat club in Moscow. Red lights were flashing, and "Back That Ass Up" was playing five years too late, or two vodkas too early. My friend Jane was grinding on the dance floor with a cute Russian guy she'd just met.

At the bar I tried to make eye contact with a guy—any guy—but it wasn't working. Jane motioned for me to come dance with her, but I didn't feel like being a third wheel. I smiled and waved, stayed at the bar, and spent the next half-hour fidgeting with my massive curly hair, trying to smooth it out, tuck in the flyaway frizz, and pull it back into an inconspicuous bun, over and over again. I wiped some condensation off my cocktail glass and used it to "gel" some curls behind my ears, so they wouldn't look like sideburns. I'd been told that I looked like a Hasidic boy with *payot,* and Jane seemed to agree.

Three hours earlier, Jane and I were at home in our warm, Soviet-block-style apartment, getting ready to go out. I was in my room, surveying my three pairs of jeans. I picked my favorite dark pair to wear over my wool tights (it was still zero degrees Fahrenheit in March), and then I put on my standby red tank top and black cardigan. Having been raised in Central Texas, I'd never worn wool tights under my jeans before.

I peered into Jane's room next door. She wore a sparkly gold top that flaunted her breasts, between which a silver necklace had been swallowed up. Her jeans were vacuum-sealed onto her body and her dirty-blond hair was silky smooth. She leaned into her mirror, expertly applying foundation to her blemish-free face.

"Oh my God, is that what you're wearing?" Jane asked with pleading eyes.

"Yeah...why?"

"Those pants are too big, you look like a stick."

"Do I?" I asked, twisting around to check out my own butt.

"Very heroin chic."

Jane started on her eyeliner, and I knew that in her own sweet way, she was just trying to help me. She wanted me on the dance floor too, with my own date. Jane was my only real friend in Moscow, and I was hers. We moved there together for an internship (a semester of administrative work for an orchestra), and neither of us was good at speaking Russian. We relied heavily on each other. I'd try to translate labels for her at the grocery store, and she'd share her DVDs, all thankfully undubbed in their original English. I'd locate a decent English-language bookstore, and she'd make me laugh when gusts of arctic wind knocked me over.

"Forget your pants, we need to finally do something about your hair," Jane added.

"Like what?" I asked, my muscles tensing as I leaned against the doorframe.

"Like straighten it. Have you ever done that?"

"Yes, it was horrible. It looked like a Halloween wig for a witch's costume."

"Well, it looks like a rat's nest the way it is. Your choice."

"Ooh, I have a choice!"

Yes, my hair was unruly sometimes. It was very curly, thick, dark brown, and it looked different every single day. Humidity turned it into a full-on afro, but not a cute symmetrical one that had been styled appropriately. Dry air turned it into a frizzy "rat's nest." Rain and snow weren't good either.

"Jane, I'm doing the best I can. I've got ten pounds of hair product in there—if you lit a match, my head would burst into flames."

"Well, it's not working."

"I can't actually *change* my hair; I can only try to control it. You know my mother's black, and black hair is totally different from hair like yours."

"I've never even seen your mother."

I went into my room and pulled out a photo of my parents. My mother sat with regal posture on a park bench next to my father, who's white with a mustache and a gentle smile. Mom had what my father called a "cream in your coffee" complexion and very short black hair, a broad nose, a strong jaw line, and the cheekbones of a queen.

"She's not even really black. Get over it and fix your hair," Jane said, handing the photo back to me.

"What?"

"She's not even, like, black-black."

"What's black-black?"

"You know."

"Well, her whole family is black, even if they're not black enough to impress you."

Jane shrugged and went to her closet to find her high-heeled boots. I continued to stand in the doorway and thought back on other people's reactions to my mother's appearance. Some people didn't realize she was black, because in truth, she had an exotic face—they thought maybe she was Cherokee or Mexican or whatever came to mind. People's reactions to my appearance varied too. Many black people recognized my roots, but others guessed that I was Puerto Rican, Jamaican, or even Egyptian, depending on how good my tan was at the time. Spanish people guessed Spanish, Jewish people guessed Jewish, and so on. When someone asked my mother that blunt, recurring question "What *are* you?" she once said, "I'm a real piece of Americana."

My mother didn't talk much about her past, but slowly over the years, I learned enough to figure out where I came from. In 1939 my mother was born in Lexington, Mississippi, which was a dangerous, segregated community. To escape, her family moved up to Detroit during the Great Migration, where my grandfather found work on a Chrysler assembly line. That couldn't have been easy, and I was proud to have such determination in my lineage.

I wandered back into my bedroom and flopped onto my bed, to think about how my rat's nest was chasing all the Russian men away. The fact that no one in Moscow shared my hair type certainly exacerbated my insecurities. In three months, I'd only seen two people of color: a black woman attending a symphony orchestra concert and a black man dressed as a piece of chocolate, passing out flyers for a nearby candy shop. On top of that, it was very popular for Russian women to dye their hair blond or red. It appeared that Anglo Saxon hair was attractive and black hair was not.

The following Friday night, Jane and I were getting ready to go out again. So I stood in front of the bathroom mirror and made a decision. Instead of trying to force my hair into submission with all of my "damaged hair" products, gallons of which I brought with me from the U.S., I would just wear it down and leave it alone. I wanted to make peace with my asymmetry, coarse frizz, and errant baby hairs. Jane didn't say anything, maybe because she'd given up, maybe because it looked better than the previous weekend, or maybe because I'd finally taken a crucial step toward being myself.

Jane and I went to a local bar this time. There was a small dance floor in the middle and a handful of cream-colored tables under green lights along the edge of the room. Jane and I stripped off our bulky winter coats and ordered a plate of pickled vegetables with two shots of vodka.

Two Russian guys at another table saw us unaccompanied and came over. Slava introduced himself in broken English, along with his friend, who didn't say a word, and they sat down and ordered some more vodka. Slava was a 30-something journalist for a local paper, covering human-interest stories, something about bicycles, and after some time, I realized that Slava was talking to *me*. He looked at Jane every now and then, but he was mostly checking *me* out. And despite my urges, I hadn't been fidgeting with my hair, or trying to fix it, all night.

Slava was not what I'd call an Adonis. His greasy, stringy black hair was pulled back into a low ponytail, his teeth were in total disarray, and he was wearing blue tinted sunglasses indoors. But who cared? Another round of vodka shots was ordered, a Russian slow jam came on, and Slava asked me to dance. We went onto the floor with a handful of other couples, leaving Jane at the table with Slava's silent friend, and it wasn't long before Slava and I were making out, arms wrapped around each other. I'm sure it wasn't pretty, but the positive attention was intoxicating. He was even gently stroking my hair.

It was already 3:00 A.M., so I said goodnight to Slava and walked home with Jane. I'd had too much to drink, so in a somewhat orderly fashion, I went into our bathroom and threw up. But I was happy, kneeling there on the bathroom floor. Someone thought I was pretty and it made me appreciate my hair the way it was.

Down the hall I could hear Jane on the phone with her sister back in the States.

"Oh my God, it was the most repulsive thing I've ever seen. She managed to find *the* ugliest guy on the planet and made out with him, in front of everyone!"

I was O.K. with that. And in that weird moment, in which I loved my hair, I felt closer to my mother and felt great about being a real piece of Americana.

Sarah Enelow grew up on mesquite barbecue and barrel racing in rural Texas. Then she lived in Indiana for two years before moving to New York City all by her lonesome. Sarah has contributed to three NYC guidebooks for Not For Tourists and wrote the first NYC guidebook for Go! Girl Guides. Sarah is only one year away from becoming a "real New Yorker." This story was previously published by Ducts.org.

KASHA RIGBY

The Bone Breaker

Today's Mayan special; a fracture of the price.

FACE DOWN IN THE DIRT, I GASPED AND TWISTED AWAY FROM the sharp gouging in my back and ribs. Tears left muddy trails down my face and blended with the hard dirt floor of the shack. This tiny withered crone—the village bone healer—had come highly recommended. She couldn't have weighed as much as 90 pounds, but she was doing the damage of a tackling linebacker.

I was alone and far from anything familiar. Blind faith had landed me here, face down in the dirt, stifling the desire to beg for mercy. I had drifted south to Guatemala after wandering Mexico's Mayan kingdom. There'd never been a plan to stay anywhere long but stops stretched and my drift south slowed until motion all but halted on the banks of this lake. I woke each morning and feigned purpose. I studied Spanish and Mayan astrology, explored coffee plantations, and dabbled with psychedelic mushrooms. I walked and swam for hours each day. I lived out of a satchel. My dirty jeans hung baggy, and the heartache that propelled me to this place faded to a dull ache.

But a physical pain had remained deep in my back. It crept down my legs, a constant discomfort. Constant motion had been the best remedy over the years. I rarely sat long, walked everywhere, and visited healers of all kinds. I distrusted Western medicine to the point of it being a phobia. And I had restless bones, not to be confused with Restless Legs, which is a syndrome. My solution to pain was motion, just as my solution to harsh words was getting on airplanes.

Many cultures have a tradition of the bone healer or bone setter, *hueseros*, in Central America. The Mayans were scientists and spiritualists. They were astronomers and architects. They performed cranial surgeries, built magnificent temples, and set teeth with jade and obsidian.

When I went to the bone setter I'd expected maybe some rough massage. I hadn't even known that I was in a town known for a specific lineage of bone healers. Most are known to be from a more empirical background, but in this village the roots were divination. The skill was said often to come forth in a dream and a tool would appear, a bone, or stone which the healer used like a divining rod, to find the root of the problem.

It was my Spanish teacher who suggested the old woman and took me to her village of dusty streets and plastic flowers, wily dogs and scrappy roosters. A two-story wall in town donned a mural of Jesus in his great glory entitled "*Jesus es el Hombre.*" That's right. Jesus is the Man.

I'd entered her home in the blinding transition of going from bright light to dark. Eyes need time to adjust, the pupils to grow. If only the entire human organism could adjust to circumstances with such a blink of the eye. A single hanging bulb revealed the house was one room with a wooden bed. There was a chest with one drawer, upon which rested two photos with faded faces staring, unlit candles, and a bottle. I tried to explain my reasons for coming, and with few words she sent me to lie on the bed stomach down. She lifted my shirt and started running her hands on my back. I could feel her palms, fingers, and knuckles so sharp. It wasn't until later that I realized she had this tool that she was also guiding along my gaunt back.

I could have misunderstood her. Our Spanish was about equal, her language was Q'eqchi'. It was with hand gestures she led me to understand that my ribs had been broken (this I knew) and had never healed straight (this I didn't know). Years earlier I had taken a hard hit from a surfboard—first wave, first day, an accident that broke my ribs and left me with a long-lasting fear of short surfboards. But I'd come to her for help with the chronic pain in my back and legs. She decided it was all from my ribs. I knew they were unrelated, but who could argue with powers from the dream world?

I was forewarned that this would be strong work, that it would hurt, but give me a shaman over a Western doctor. I wanted generations of healers passed on to me through her bony knuckles. The long strokes turned to a deeper rough gouging, first on top of my ribs and then channeling between my ribs. I called upon years of yoga practice breath work. I tried to keep steady and calm. If I could control my breath, I could get through this. Then I was fighting and gulping. And it was over. This was my first session.

I dusted off my market-purchased skirt that I wrapped over my jeans—the uniform of the practical and tough fem. I pulled in a deep ragged breath, wiped dirty tears from my face, and handed over my worn bills that smelled of the passing of unwashed hands—the physical representation of "dirty money." I scheduled my return in two days.

Back at the hostel, I cracked a cold beer early to down a renegade Valium. This was not the day to curse the charlatan pharmaceutical companies. My breath labored. I had rented a simple room. All the rooms had a small porch and opened up to a big courtyard with a shared outdoor kitchen. We were a haphazard little tribe that had landed here. We formed casual friendships that arose quickly and often disappeared just as fast. We set a long table at night and took turns going to the market and making big wholesome meals. There were always crates of tall beer bottles. Some folks were here on break from service projects, others just on breaks from life.

My scheduled return to the old woman approached, and with apprehension I gave myself plenty of time for the walk over. I arrived in the village that afternoon dreading the work to come but hopeful that the short pain would offer long-term relief.

She was ready for me when I entered. She shooshed out several children and got right to business. Today the power must have been out as candles were lit to add to the filtered light entering through two windows. The bed didn't have a mattress but instead stacks of worn blankets. I lifted up my shirt and lay face down. At first she used long strokes with oil along my ribs. I hoped today would be easier. There was a peaceful minute. Then the digging began. I was unsure if she was using her fingers or something else. It was only later that I confirmed she used a bone or stone. She always kept it hidden in her hand. I tried not to cry out, but it felt like my ribs were splintering like a fiberglass boat. No, I was sure they were. She was breaking my ribs! How could she be delivering such brutality? I twisted away gasping. I found it difficult to move and could hardly get up after she'd finished. Again, tears streaked my cheeks, as I handed her more dirty money. I was scared to say "no" when she said I must come back one more time "*manana.*"

My only stop on the way back to my touristy village was the *farmacia*, to beg the skeptical woman behind the counter to sell me more diazepam without a prescription. Money talks in Guatemala and I exited with a fresh supply. Speaking to no one, I bee-lined to the safety of my little hole in the wall, grabbed one of those tall cold beers from our group supply, cracked it and washed down a blue pill. During the hot afternoon, I cradled the sweaty cold bottles against my side for relief, and as the sun set, I wrapped up in my one sweater and a blanket, awaiting the return of my friends, out on adventures on the lake and in other villages. So much for my dislike of Western medicine; I was happily downing modern prescriptions and beer and passed out before anyone returned to our compound.

I woke in the dark, chilled, dehydrated, hardly able to move, the moments of bravado I felt the night before, gone. I was small and tired, alone and in pain. My tongue was thick and dry. I wanted to heave but knew the pain would be unbearable. Something had not gone well in this plan. The constant aching went from prickling to spiking and no position brought relief. Wrapped in my wool blanket, I tried an upright position, waiting out the long hours for sun to rise, allowing myself one more Valium, washed down this time with gulps of water.

Finally the morning came, and I needed to put myself together. The showers and bathroom were a walk across the common courtyard, and I slipped out before hearing the rustling of others. I stood in my flip-flops in the shower for a long time, not wanting to face others or even the day, or brave going back for my afternoon appointment. I couldn't imagine even walking over, let alone the crone, the healer, laying one finger on me. I shut off the hot water while wrapped up in my sarong and headed to the kitchen.

The next to rise was another American, a musician and friend. "James, could you help me out for a sec? Do you mind looking at my back?" I turned and lowered my wrap, modesty gone.

"What the...what? What did you do?" Hearing the shock in his voice, I dragged a chair to the one mirror in the hostel (which was in the kitchen), climbed up on the chair, and executed the agonizing look back over my shoulder. A rainbow of bruises covered my back and wrapped around my sides. There were long welts, deep purple and red, running the length of my swollen ribs. I was stunned but finally got it. I'd needed the visual proof of the beating. Until this moment I thought I was not being tough enough, that if I could only just lie still and endure it, that the old woman was going to help me. But this was far worse than the original injuries.

"How many times did you go to her? And wait, how much have you been paying?" James was concerned, but I could also see he was trying to withhold laughter.

"Holy shit, I've been paying for this. I'm not going back!" He was right. There was definitely some comedy at my expense. I wouldn't see a doctor originally, and now here I was drinking beer to wash down prescription drugs because I'd been beaten by a 90-year-old, 90-pound woman.

"You're not going anywhere today kid." He kissed my forehead and started to strum his guitar, and with laughter in his eyes and on his lips, began to sing one of my favorites, "Medicine Man."

★

Kasha Rigby is a mountaineer and skier with multiple first descents. She's dubbed "the pioneer of extreme telemarking." Yet she finds navigating the planet externally seems much easier than navigating the internal mind. Kasha tries to add at least a new county, try a new job, and an unknown experience every year. This year the theme is "discipline"—physical and mental. So far this has led her to Peru, a service project in Ghana, and also to fourteen weeks sleeping in the dirt on Ultimate Survival Alaska *(National Geographic), plus skiing and looking for northern lights in Alaska. Kasha is a writer, a Kundalini yoga teacher, and is continuing to try and "do good work in this lifetime and not mess it up too bad." This takes grand effort and even more luck.*

LEANNE SHIRTLIFFE

A Tale of Two Toilets

Awkward in Ambalangoda.

WE CHOOSE AMBALANGODA WITH CARE. IT IS, AFTER ALL, the final destination of our three-week backpacking trip in Sri Lanka. Besides having a name that rolls off the tongue in a way that would please Dr. Seuss, Ambalangoda has one of the whitest beaches on the island and can serve as our one-stop-shopping destination before we depart back to the Middle East, where we've lived for nearly three years.

After we spend the afternoon debating the merits of various hand-carved masks—should we purchase the one that induces vomit, the one that creates mass amounts of bile, or the one that causes paralysis?—we walk until we find a restaurant populated with Ambalangodans. Outside the open-air structure, which leans haphazardly toward the sea, we study a pond filled with the catches of the day, trying to pick the unfortunate fish that will become our dinner. My fiancé and I soon realize that two kids from the Canadian Prairies choosing fresh seafood is the equivalent of a vegan selecting a side of beef. We settle on something that moves and has gills.

En route to our table, I ask, "Where is the toilet?"

"This way," the waiter gestures. I open the bathroom door, step over the threshold and see the slippery squat toilet—two porcelain footprints that rise out of the floor, surrounded by murky liquid. My bladder begs me to go forth, but my sandal-clad feet stop midstride. I can't do this tonight. I'm embarrassed that my sense of adventure has vanished. It's our last night. Is not getting my feet wet too much to ask? I opt to hold my pee, bladder infection be damned.

The waiter observes my about-face. "Come," he says, "I'll show you a Western toilet. Much better for you."

Sheepishly, I follow—through the kitchen, out the back door, across the alley, up the street, and into a tailor shop. We climb a flight of stairs into a second-story family home.

Before exiting stage left, the waiter explains my situation to the homeowner, a woman clad in an "I love Pepsi" t-shirt and a colorful batik sarong. I watch their banter and am dumbstruck. My hostess smiles at me, nods encouragingly, and proceeds to bang on a closed door, shouting in Sinhalese. A male voice, also yelling, answers. A shower provides the soundtrack to this cacophony.

"No. No. Really. It's O.K.," I stutter. "I'll go."

Smiling again, the woman guides me to an empty room, carries in a plastic patio chair, and motions for me to sit. I couldn't feel more awkward if I tried.

While my hostess pleads through the bathroom door, I gaze out the window, over rooftops and toward the sea and the setting sun. I recall other Sri Lankan bathrooms, such as a dark hut outside a tourism shop in Kandy. Armed with hiking boots, a day's supply of single-ply toilet paper, antibacterial wipes, coins for a possible sur- charge and the prerequisite courage, I hover precariously over the toilet-hole—only to notice a hairy spider the

size of a softball creeping my way. It's a freaking tarantula. My body freezes, my heart accelerates, and a stare-
down ensues. I flashback to a nightmare my grandmother
shared with me when I was a girl: a tarantula had sat
on her cheek while she slept, hatched eggs in her skin,
and baby tarantulas crawled out from her mouth. In the
forever of this real-life moment of me squatting next to
a tarantula, my bowels empty. Then empty some more.
Nature's enema works quickly.

The next week, I narrowly avert peeing on a python.
I step off the hiking trail, crouch into a practiced squat,
and urinate. As I yank up my shorts, I hear a rustling mere
feet in front of me. A full-size python slithers out from the
underbrush toward the path. My flight-or-fight response
activates, I do neither: I freeze.

Later that same night, after imbibing two extra large
bottles of Lion Stout while sitting on our bed, I realize
that our mosquito net has a hole in it. So I do what any
fertile woman would do: I grab a maxi pad (with wings),
peel off the wrapper, and stick it to the mesh. The lone
light bulb dangling from the ceiling projects a six-foot
shadow onto the wall—with wings. It's a Kotex moment
that still gives me night sweats.

My vacation reverie is interrupted. I shift in my plastic
chair and hear more shouting, followed by the opening
of the bathroom door. A twenty-something Sri Lankan
man emerges, dripping wet, with a towel clinging to his
waist. He snaps at his mother, then turns to me with a
grin. "I'm so sorry," he says, apologizing for showering in
his own bathroom.

"No. I'm so sorry," I say. We continue our mutual
apologies as he scurries past my chair. We are both self-
conscious—him for being semidressed and for showering when a spoiled tourist needs a special toilet, and me

for invading his house, his bathroom, and his privacy. We acknowledge the awkwardness with smiles.

I clamber into the washroom and see the Western toilet partly submerged in shower suds. The water swirls over my feet, snaking into a drain. I squat over the soaked toilet and shake my head at the irony.

I struggle to exit gracefully, leaving sopping footprints in my wake. I thank my hostess profusely and apologize for having no money.

She shakes her head saying, "No money."

The dusky Ambalangodan breeze greets me as I wander downhill, in what I hope is the direction of the restaurant. The sun doesn't waste time setting in the tropics, and the shadowy backdoors of several businesses look similar. Eventually I open the correct door, smile at the restaurant's kitchen staff, and spy my fiancé. A barbecued open-eyed fish and our carved vomit mask flank him. He looks worse than both.

"Are you O.K.?" he asks. "Where the heck have you been?"

"In the bathroom." I sit down on the patio chair and smile at the beer my fiancé has ordered for me.

"All this time?" he asks. "I've seen several people go and return from the bathroom since you left."

"Oh," I say. "Well, I wasn't in *this* bathroom."

He pauses, gulps his Lion Stout. "Which bathroom were you in?"

I glance down at our catch-of-the-day and see its glassy eye staring at me. I refocus on my fiancé, momentarily thankful he has two eyes. "I went to someone's house to use their toilet."

"You went to someone's house? By yourself?"

"No, of course not." I chuckle at the idiocy of that suggestion. "I followed the waiter out the back."

As if on cue, the waiter arrives. My fiancé orders a second beer. I move the vomit mask and start scooping out fish flesh.

My fiancé says, "Why in God's name would you follow the waiter into someone's house?"

"I didn't want a squat toilet. I was tired of getting my feet wet. Of course, when the man came out of the shower, the toilet and the floor were completely soaked, so I might as well have peed here."

"What *man in the shower*?"

I sip my warmish beer. "The lady's son. The lady whose house it was."

I retell the story in greater detail while we eat our fish. We laugh at the absurdity of it all, at my urinary missteps, and at the uncalled-for generosity of the Sri Lankan people who—in spite of the war-torn north of their country and the widespread poverty—are happy to oblige a desperate woman with weird bathroom habits.

Leanne Shirtliffe is the author of Don't Lick the Minivan, The Change Your Name Store, *and* Mommyfesto. *She has won a caber-toss championship in Bahrain and has chased transvestites in Bangkok—in order to get advice on buying shoes. Leanne, her former fiancé, and their twins now live in Calgary, Alberta, because they like complaining about the weather. Read more about their (mis)adventures at IronicMom.com*

Spanking It in the South Pacific

The Fiji of nobody's dreams.

THE TRANSFER BOAT IS TINY, LEAKS, IS MANNED BY A MAN with 32 consonants in his name and has no life preservers. It is a death craft. It pulls off land, and for the next 30 minutes we alternate between horizontal and vertical, depending on which wave is most determined to flip us. Poseidon blasts a gusher of a wave, which flings us within view of Yaqeta Island. The boat operator begins to look less terrified as we approach land and downright relieved when he's able to drop me off on the shore.

I picked this island because it was off the books. Too late for a quarter-life crisis and too soon for the big midlife, I tried to find the balance between a packaged backpacker tour and one of those adventures where people hire Sherpas, climb steep mountains, and clink off their frostbitten toes. I was often called a "pussy" in high school and can now freely admit that this is a fair tag. This pussy wanted a manageable extreme experience.

Upon arrival, a glance proved that the tip I'd been given was right: this is more of an outpost than anything else. I didn't expect anyone else to be here, but am greeted by one other tourist who is happy to see new company, even if it is a pale man from Manhattan

John is a 22-year-old Asian American from Connecticut. He has zero percent body fat and a visible six-pack, presumably from training for every Olympic sport simultaneously.

Let me explain the *resort*. There are seven leaky shacks on a beach, none with electricity and all with spiders the size of Pam Anderson's left tit. We live in shack number two, which has ten bunk beds. My bed is seven millimeters from John's, and I worry that my body fat will encroach onto his perfectly sculpted frame. He is *Men's Health and Fitness* and I am the TGI Friday's menu.

There is a pillow on my bed made of cast iron and a sheet that was woven by people without fingers. There is nothing comfortable about Yaqeta. Then 10 minutes later I am snorkeling and see the same fish that I usually only witness in my stoner friends' aquariums.

John and I eat some island made potato-ramen combo and drink bottled water that has been refilled and sold as if it is new. The generator runs out of fuel around 9:00. I take an Ambien to block out the mosquitoes buzzing around my bed's shoddy net and sleep blissfully until the end-of-the-world rain starts pummeling our hut at 6:00, just an hour before the breakfast conch is blown with great inexperience. After seven trumpeted notes of what sounds like a dying ferret, John echoes my thoughts. "We get the point."

John has been alone on the island for two days and follows me around like a retriever. He is in the Navy ROTC and speaks military talk ("copy that"). I make a mental note to get him drunk and ask what really happens when sailors are at sea for months. I have seen porn with this theme and hope it is just as good.

We go to the village with Michael, who takes care of our resort. There are huts and roosters and dogs and kids running around, and nobody is speaking anything other than Fijian. I only understand *bula,* which means hello.

We visit a school and see knives stuck in coconuts, sleeping adults lying face first on the floor, and a large color picture of Cher. There are lessons about Japan on a chalkboard. The board reads, "The Japanese are rich. They live in big houses."

We leave the school and I nearly collide with a cow that looks like Al Gore. Our eyes lock.

On the way back we stop at the funeral of a woman who was 92. She is being buried in the sand, and all of the kids are tossing dirt on her. I am asked to toss dirt on her. Then I am asked to help shovel dirt on her. I am burying a 92-year-old Fijian woman.

I walk back to the resort with an older man who tells me that he has a mole. I tell him that's nice. He turns to show me something resembling a puss-filled red golf ball on his chest. I hold back the vomit and expect him to be dead in hours. He just shrugs and keeps walking. If I had a mole like that I would have 50 people praying for me in the ICU at St. Vincent's. But this dude, he's *gotta* go take care of the goats now.

Everything gets surreal after this, as if it wasn't already. The rain doesn't stop. Michael wants us to go to the village for lunch. I agree. When we arrive, the village is in full funeral party mode. I say hi to Al Gore on the way in, and he gives me a nasty look.

We watch men pound kava root—*boring.* We watch men drink kava root—*boring.* We sit on fly-covered blue tarps while the men talk about the dead lady in Fijian for an hour—sorry lady, but *booooring.* Then we sit in a man's fly-filled hut while he tries to push pork at me, which is only made worse by the fact that the pig's head is lying on the ground outside.

John and I beg to be let out of this Fijian hell and start toward the beach, calculating how much fly poo each of us has had deposited on our skin. Then I see it. It was not something I was ready for. They are slaughtering Al Gore!

He's moping around slowly as his belly is falling out. The crowd around him seems glad that he is dying. He falls. And then Al Gore is dead, hogtied to a stake, and is carried off by two of the island's strongest men. I skip the festival of death and return to the huts.

John and I play cards with newly arrived Brits, who greatly resemble The Ropers. Joe, the husband, has been sick. *That* kind of sick. This will be Joe's last trip around the world. His wife is incredibly fun and upbeat and wears a tie-dye sarong and tells me about seeing Pink Floyd at the first Glastonbury Festival. I'm hoping she will adopt me. I want to live with her in Bath and go down to the pub with her every day and have a discreet relationship with a man named Philip who will either work at the steel mill or the local arts and crafts store. Several whiskeys later the generator quits. John and I stumble to our bunkroom.

But here's the thing—I have to jack off. I mean really. I have not gone this long since I was 15 years old. John is asleep or maybe listening to headphones. I am buzzed on the Jack Daniels we've been drinking, and I just don't care any more. I consider a trip to the bathroom to take care of it but can't shake the image of a snake coiling around my dick in the dark like a venomous cock ring. Also, it is dark in the room, and I have the mosquito net around me that operates as a wall. This is how I rationalize things when I have this much semen inside of me.

I do this wristy thing because I can't rapid-move with John so close. It's a slow movement with subtle flare and major style points at pivotal moments. I make fast work of it. Four things happen quickly: 1) I blast buckets and buckets. 2) I suppress the biggest moan of my life so far on this planet. 3) I look around overwhelmed with the amount of fluid, unsure of what protocol is. 4) I fall asleep.

I wake at dawn, looking at two semen drips, semi-crystallized from the hours that have passed, hanging from the mosquito net. The morning sunrise is hitting them at an angle that can only be described as beautiful—an orgasm stalactite.

It's our last day on Yaqeta. We have seven hours to kill between breakfast and the boat transfer. There is nothing to do. I pace the beach and Energy Boy climbs a rock, building further muscle mass. We eat and then climb into the boat. John is going back to Connecticut, and I am off to a new island. We are both excited to leave Yaqeta behind us. Also we've been talking about pizza, and John has that near-narcotic extra-cheese look in his eye.

Then it all goes wrong. The sound of a boat engine dying is not very dramatic: a couple of pings, a sputter. We drift. We use a pole to get back to the beach. We nearly cry. We will miss the *big boat*. We are angry. We stew. We do not say "thank you" when they upgrade us to a hut with its own bathroom and wasps that coexist in the ceiling with mice. This will be a miserable night.

John takes what he calls an "angry swim," and I hike an hour to the top of the mountain, because I heard if you do two back flips while praying you can get cell service. No luck. You just get goats that run away so fast they fall down—probably because you are throwing rocks to get them off the path. I contemplate putting my Blackberry into an apple juice bottle and setting it out to sea, my last plea for help as the island sucks my soul into its sand. I've gone to a level of melodrama that only a teenager with mononucleosis would understand.

John and I collect loads of wood. Our concept is that the only thing that will make us happy now is a fire that you can see from Mars. The locals look at us like we are nutso as we discuss how we don't know if bamboo will burn, but gee, doesn't it look just like the sake containers at Nobu? Everything we pile onto the fire burns big and bright.

Our transfer boat works the next day, and we make the big boat on time. We laugh, relieved.

I say goodbye to John. I know how this goes. We exchange email addresses and make claims to keep in touch, but won't. For three days and four luxurious nights we were best friends, yet if we'd passed each other in a hallway back home, we wouldn't have given each other a second glance. In the real world we're probably not each other's kind of guys, but out here on Yaqeta we were travel brothers. It's not every week you get stranded on an island, watch a vice president get slaughtered, and light a fire that you can see from Mars.

★

Tom Gates is the author of the best-selling independent book Wayward: Fetching Tales from a Year on the Road. *He has served as an editor at Matador Network, where he has reported from five continents over six years. Gates has also had a remarkable career in the music industry, working over 20 years with artists who have sold over 50 million combined albums, including Christina Perri, fun!, Coldplay, Patti Smith, Dido, and Santana.*

Biannual Belgian Blowout

*"I just implied that she was a little hippy...though she
has got the biggest potamus I've ever seen."*
—Lucy Ricardo

MY RIGHT EYE THROBBED IN ITS SOCKET, AND WHEN I SMILED
a small spot on the lower lid pinched like a bee sting.

"Then don't smile," said the doctor.

He examined the purple puffy skin, pushing and mas-
saging with his thumb in a circular pattern while looking
over the top of the bifocals that rested on the end of his
bulbous nose.

I flinched.

"How did this happen?" he asked.

I wanted to tell him that I've ice-picked up a frozen
waterfall, been tossed from a rubber raft in an icy river,
rode a bucking horse through the back country of Yellow-
stone National Park, and have zip-lined, mountain biked,
SCUBA'd and skied around the planet. I couldn't tell him
how I'd really sustained my injury. I'd have to lie. Yes, I'd
definitely lie.

I arrived at the mall early on a wintery Saturday morning during The Sales (Les Soldes) to beat the rush, but the mall had actually opened one hour before. Minus the camping out overnight, it was the equivalent of our Black Friday on steroids.

Wilting shoppers slumped over café counters, bringing dollhouse-sized porcelain espresso cups to their lips in unison, tossing their heads back in a choreographed, whiplash-inducing motion. They perked up like newly watered plants then stepped back into the mall melee. Only an IV drip feed could have caffeinated them faster. These retail warriors pinballed from store to store, nudging me out of the way with their sharp elbows and heaving irritated French lip puffs toward my ear, noises I interpreted as "speed up or get out of the way, lady." Weighty bags dangled from their wrists and bent arms like tree ornaments. One woman blurred by me pushing a stroller piled with shoeboxes and throw pillows. Her crying toddler son kept pace, his flat feet motoring in rhythmic circular slaps reminiscent of Fred Flintstone in his bottomless car.

In many ways, Europeans are more civilized than us Yanks across the Atlantic. Long lunches, work-free Sundays, and four weeks of vacation a year are just a few pieces of evidence to support that claim. But come January and July, the temptation to nab name brands at rock-bottom prices turns them into credit card-slinging warriors who would make our heroes of the Wild West tremble. My French teacher had delivered a prophetic clue when, weeks earlier while discussing the biannual blowouts, she'd raised her eyebrow and said, "Normally our sales are very different from yours." She (like all Francophones do when speaking English) used the word "normally" in the curious way that imbues us Anglophones with feelings of hopeful doubt, as in "normally this doesn't hurt" or "normally this should hold the roof up." The word "normally" was my tip-off.

I ducked into Inno, a department store I liked and had browsed in once before. Under the garish fluorescent lights, women young and old hunkered over a bin of bargain accessories like feral cats feeding at crab carcasses. One squeezed her Rubenesque fingers into a red leather glove one size too small while another foraged for matching socks, tossing castoffs into the air like confetti. Nearby, glass display cases were lifeless bone yards, drained of their contents while rejected necklaces, earrings, rings, and watches lay strewn over countertops. I spun the sunglass carousel a couple of quarter turns before removing a retro, cat-eye pair, and slid the rigid arms behind my ears. I squinted into a miniscule, blurry mirror and hoped an Audrey Hepburn-like face would peer back. Instead, a white paper tag hooked with plastic to the bridge between the lenses dangled down the length of my freckled nose. I held the tag up and out of the way, and leaned in. *Maybe*, I thought. I set the glasses down on the counter next to the other sale corpses.

I had initially shrugged off "doing" the sales, as my French teacher had suggested a few weeks earlier. In America, I'd told her, sales were going on all the time. What's the big deal? When she told me Les Soldes were like the Olympics of retail and that items were discounted up to 70 percent off, images of gold medals in the shape of euro symbols popped up in little bubbles above my head. One thing I'd admired since moving to Brussels was the manner in which men and women dressed. Whether going to the weekly *marché*, a fine restaurant, or picking up the ubiquitous dog crap that littered the street, these ladies and gents looked amazing, as if they'd just stepped off the glossy covers of *Haute Shopping Magazine* and *Dog Shit*

Collectors Quarterly. Often in heels, always a scarf tied just so, manicured nails that never chipped, maybe a sexy pair of dangling earrings to catch the light, European women embodied an effortless chic style I coveted. Most days I wore (*quelle horreur*) stretchy yoga pants. No self-respecting European woman would ever wear stretchy yoga pants out in public—unless she was actually going to a yoga class. After months of feeling like the archetypal "Fashion Don't," I decided to revitalize my American bore-drobe by adding in some scarves and skirts, and Les Soldes were just the place to start.

On the way to women's clothing on the second floor, I lollygagged through lingerie, fingering the delicate intimates. I stepped on the escalator just in time to see a woman reach for a black bra. Then another woman reached for the same bra. One tugged, the other jerked, and each screeched until the louder and stronger of the two stumbled backward, her lacy prize clutched to her chest, and swaggered like a newly crowned prize fighter to the fitting room while the other sulked away empty handed. If Charles Darwin had been there, he'd have smiled seeing his theory of natural selection alive and well and living the dream in women's underwear. Like trained sportsmen or pilgrims setting out along the Santiago de Compostela, these shoppers were prepared physically and mentally. I pictured them at home stretching and doing finger push-ups for weeks in advance, or squeezing those rubber stress balls while chanting a bargain hunter's mantra in front of a shrine set up in the closet. *I am the fastest, strongest, deadliest shopper alive. Oooooohhhhhmmmm.*

A friend of mine, who'd been living in Brussels for a couple of years when we met, confirmed that there is, in fact, some preparation involved. "I go out on reconnaissance missions ahead of time," she'd told me over lunch. "I try things on so I know exactly which sizes I need, then all

I have to do is run into the store and buy them." Reconnaissance missions? Really?

Upstairs, shoppers groped at rounders of blouses, and stacked wooden cubes were stuffed pell-mell with jeans and t-shirts. A half-dozen women swarmed a rack of wool and down coats that bulged underneath a red-and-white 60 percent off sign. It might as well have been a lantern attracting moths to the flame. In one of the trendier departments, a young female store clerk delicately unbuttoned the leather jacket of a headless mannequin, pulled it off the shoulders, and removed the mannequin's right arm along with it. The clerk wrestled with the arm, eventually putting it between her legs for leverage and finally relieved the jacket sleeve of the cumbersome appendage just as I approached her to ask where I could find the skirts. She pointed with the white plastic arm toward the next section and walked away, jacket and arm in hand.

The skirts were packed together on a rack as tight as library books. I pried them apart with the outside of my hands in search of tags and my size. A bulky woman next to me pushed the skirts back, forcing my hands closed. I spread my hands open again, glancing at her sideways. She returned daggers and shoved the hangers back toward me with a quick, squeaky jerk. So went this folly until I managed to liberate a skirt. From the other side of the rack, a woman strode quickly toward me, her black high heels clip-clopping on the scuffed-up tile floor. Without making eye contact, and despite us being only inches apart, she shuffled through the skirts faster than a Vegas blackjack dealer. The hangers whined against the metal bar until she realized I was staring at her, and she stopped.

"Which size is that?" she finally asked me in French, pointing to the skirt I'd been holding in my hand.

"Thirty-eight," I replied.

"That's the one I am looking for," she said, reaching for it over the rack.

On any other day, I might have just given her the skirt. But somewhere between the feral cats at the accessory bin and the bra boxing match one floor below, a competitive spirit had sprouted inside me like a weed. The second this woman reached across the rack, the game was on and the skirt became the coveted gold medal. It was mine!

"Oh, I'm not putting it back, I'm trying it on," I smirked, letting the hanger oscillate on my middle finger like a hypnotist's watch. "But if it doesn't fit, I'll put it back."

Her arm snapped to her side, her chest inflated, and she pursed her lips, pushing out a puff of air through her flared nostrils, like an angry bull. She looked prissy in her pressed blue jeans and long-sleeved blouse capped with white Peter Pan collar. Her dyed and lacquered blond hair with matching pink cheeks and lipstick had the opposite effect of their youthful intention, and she appeared much older than she probably was. Still, she looked me up and down, toe to head, passing judgment on my American attire of sensible (comfortable) shoes, stretch pants (no excuse), and baggy sweater (ugly bra underneath). She stared at my uncoiffed hair. I batted my mascara-less eyelashes at her.

"*Excusez-moi Madame.*" She continued in English, having quickly deciphered my nationality, "But I have come back just for that skirt."

Aha! A real live *reconnoitrisse!*

"Well, I guess you should have come back a little earlier then," I retorted in my thickest, rude American accent. If I'd had chewing gum in my mouth, I'd have blown a bubble.

The blond woman glared at me over the rack. I glared back. The other women at the skirt rack slid hangers back and forth below our noses, unaware of the imminent high-noon showdown. I turned on my rubber heels and walked away. No way was I heading straight for the dressing room either!

At a table of tangled sweaters, I wedged my way in and picked through them, holding up one at a time, turning it slowly, petting sleeves, and fondling buttons. I unearthed a black cardigan that I held against the skirt. The blond woman eyeballed me from across the table. I put the sweater over my arm and sauntered past a few racks of dresses, letting my fingers touch and feel every one. The line for the register was 20 deep, and I cut through the middle, pardoning myself in front of a woman holding a pile of clothes that reached her chin. The skirt stalker followed close behind. At a stack of hats and scarves, I rubbed the various fabrics between my fingers. Silk. Merino wool. Polyester blend. I tied a floral red-and-blue scarf around my neck, then pulled on a cream-colored cashmere beret, tucking my bright red hair behind my ears and setting the beret slightly askew on my head. The blond woman's heels clicked to a halt behind me. I turned.

"*Bonjour Madame,*" I said in my best French accent, raising my eyebrows up and down à la Pépé Le Pew.

"*S'il. Vous. Plait. Madame,*" she said, hands to the heavens, "you are being very rude."

Moi? Rude? I pulled off the hat but kept the scarf on and quickened my pace. I was going to lose this broad!

The blond woman's clicking heels sounded like shuffling cards as she tried to catch up. For a change I was happy to be wearing running shoes. I had the advantage. I bolted, zig-zagging between racks of hideous holiday sweaters, ducking behind an unattended cashier desk, and finally tucking in behind the headless mannequin whose arm I'd seen severed earlier. I rested my head and scarf on top of the plastic torso and held out my right arm, filling the gap where the missing limb once dangled. I shifted my eyes left to right and waited for the blond woman. I envisioned her stopping right in front of the mannequin, turning and spinning, scratching her head, oblivious to my ruse, then skulking away in defeat—just how it's done in the movies. After several minutes and no sign of her, however, I pulled my head off the mannequin and swaggered toward the fitting room, proud of my clever victory.

Unlike most stores in America where dressing rooms are often located in a separate space, usually at the back of the store, this one was in the middle of the floor, a set of eight simple stalls, four facing one way, four facing the other, divided by thin walls, with heavy, black canvas curtains for doors. I was whistling the *Chariots of Fire* theme song when my puckered lips fell.

"I'll wait right here," the blonde said.

Her arms were crossed and her right foot tapped like a patent-leather metronome in front of the only open dressing room.

Foiled.

I stepped in and watched her smirk disappear as I pulled the curtain closed. When I turned to the mirror, I saw an arm propped in the corner, presumably the same plastic arm the clerk carried away earlier. Its fingers were up, palm facing me, as if it were waving.

"*Bonjour!*" I waved back.

I tried on the sweater first, unbuttoning it, slipping it on sleeve-by-sleeve, and buttoning it up at an exaggeratedly unhurried paced. I pulled off my shoes and my stretch pants. Standing there in a scarf, a black cardigan, and my underwear, I pulled at the zipper of the skirt, which was a little sticky, but after a few tugs, eventually gave way. I stepped into the skirt and yanked the zipper back up. The skirt was heather gray and tulip-shaped with black trim on the scalloped hem, and made me appear taller and thinner than I actually am. It fit like a glove. I stood on my tippy-toes to mimic the heels I'd need to buy and turned like a ballerina in point shoes, admiring a 360-degree view of the skirt's curve-hugging form. I curtsied to myself in front of the mirror and then to the arm. "Oh, why thank you," I said, pressing my hand to my chest. "Yes, yes, I do look good don't I?... Oh, stop, you're too kind."

"Well?" the woman called from outside the curtain, breaking my reverie.

"Well," I mouthed silently to my reflection, rolling my eyes.

I didn't answer her.

I cinched in my waist with my hands, shifting my hips side to side. I'm going to buy those cat-eye sunglasses on the way out, too. Damn, I'm going to look hot riding a Vespa through Rome!

I reached behind me for the zipper, which again stuck as I tried to pull it down, but this time it didn't budge. I held the waistband with one hand and pulled the zipper harder. No go. I spun the skirt around so the zipper was in front of me where I could see it, and pulled it again. Then, in one quick yank, even harder. The zipper split in two like the wishbone of a Thanksgiving turkey, mangling a few of its teeth for good measure. Crap. I pulled the skirt off, hung it hastily back up, and tried to zip it up again, squeezing the teeth together like puzzle pieces, hoping they'd connect long enough for me to hand off the skirt and run. I got dressed, grabbed my purse, the skirt, and, at the last second, the mannequin limb. I smiled and slid open the curtain.

"For you *Madame*," I said, extending the arm like a boo-by-trapped plastic olive branch. The skirt hanger swung on the plastic fingertips.

I guess I hadn't clipped one of the two metal clamps tight enough, and the weight of the fabric pulled the skirt from its hanger, tumbling it toward the floor.

Like a receiver anticipating the last second Hail Mary pass, she followed the garment with her eyes, bending down and snatching it out of the air centimeters from the ground. Instinctively, I'd bent over at the same time but was the slower of the two, and when she lurched up, the top of her head smacked hard into my descending cheekbone, sending me and the arm crashing to the ground, wailing in pain. The very picture of the agony of defeat.

After several minutes, I finally stopped seeing stars and sat up. I blinked until my vision focused on several shoppers and a store clerk surrounding me, their concerned looks trained on my eye, which felt as if it were dangling out of its socket on a spring. I looked around but didn't see the blond woman (or the skirt) anywhere. She was gone—vanished across the finish line with her prize without so much as an "*excusez-moi*" or "are you O.K.?" for her not-so-worthy opponent.

I stood up, the thumping in my face pulsing in time with my heartbeat, and slung my purse over my shoulder.

I wondered if I could get a discount on the arm.

After two days of resting a bag of frozen chicken nuggets on my face, I went to the doctor to find out why the swelling hadn't reduced.

Now he waited for the answer to his question as to how I sustained the contusion to my right eye.

"Well, I was climbing the Matterhorn…" I started.

He looked at me over his glasses then pushed on my eye again.

"Normally this won't hurt," he said.

That, too, was a total lie.

★

Kimberley Lovato is a freelance writer and author based in San Francisco who has admired and sometimes mimicked the antics of Lucille Ball since she dressed like her for Halloween in the seventh grade. Kimberley's travel, lifestyle, and food articles have appeared in print and online media, including National Geographic Traveler, American Way, Delta Sky, AFAR, Australian Voyeur, Marin Magazine, *travelandleisure.com, bbc.com, and more. Her culinary travel book,* Walnut Wine & Truffle Groves, *won the 2012 Gold Lowell Thomas Award given by the Society of American Travel Writers Foundation, while her essay "Lost and Liberated" received the 2012 Bronze Lowell Thomas Award as well as a Solas Award from Travelers' Tales. www.kimberleylovato.com*

SEAN O'REILLY

What I Did in the
Doll House

A special gift is left behind.

MANY YEARS AGO, I FLEW TO BOSTON TO VISIT MY BROTHER in Watertown, Massachusetts. At the time he had a wonderful barn that he had converted into a two-story office and guesthouse. The flooring downstairs was culled from the demolition of a local high school's gym, and the shelves were lined with books. Skylights completed the picture; it was a nice place and he was proud of it. He had not, however, due to restrictive local building codes installed a bathroom. On the last night of my visit, I asked that the door be left open to the main house so that I might use the bathroom should any nocturnal prompting create difficulties. I was assured that this would be done, and later I went cheerfully to bed.

I awoke early at 5:30 A.M. and although rested, felt vaguely out of focus. I attributed this to waking up in a strange place. I puttered around for 15 or 20 minutes until nature suddenly spoke loudly that big business was at hand. I moved swiftly and quietly to the door of the main house, but to my surprise and consternation discovered that the door that was supposed to be unlocked was locked. It was far too early to be waking everybody up, so I began to cast about for alternatives there at the crack, so to speak, of dawn. The bushes were not tall enough to hide the pending, disgraceful activity, and there were few trees. There were also, unfortunately, many houses nearby with their lights on and the inhabitants stirring for the morning commute. Something else was also trying to commute and communicate, and it hadn't even had its coffee yet!

My anxious and barely awake consciousness was swamped with rectal messages that alternated between desperate pleadings and the howling of possessed beasts. I looked about frantically, walking with clenched buttocks, and attempted to maintain composure in a rapidly dis-integrating situation. The standard protocols for civilized behavior were starting to break down, as they tend to in situations of extreme need. The doll house, the doll house! There was a doll house next to the barn—a bright cheer-ful thing of pink-and-yellow plastic and just large enough for an adult. I scurried inside and, pleased with my newly acquired privacy, released a tidal wave of fecal matter all over the floor. The stench was overpowering in the con-fined space of such a small area, so I made a hasty exit after performing the necessary ablutions with my t-shirt. The grotesque looseness of the still-heaving and uneven mass made me realize that it would be better if it had time to dry before I cleaned it up. I congratulated myself for find-ing a creative solution to my little problem and washed my hands at the hose. I thought no more about the matter and went back to the barn for an enjoyable hour of early morning reading.

Later that morning and before I left for the airport, I had a delightful breakfast with my brother and his family. It wasn't until I got on the plane that I realized I had made no effort to clean up the mess. My fellow passengers must have thought they had a lunatic on board as I thrashed and wheezed in my seat. All I could think about on the way to Virginia was that my brother and his wife would have to tell their young children that no, they could not use the doll house because their uncle had shat in it.

Sean O'Reilly is editor-at-large for Travelers' Tales (www.travelerstales.com). He is a former seminarian, stockbroker, and prison instructor with a degree in Psychology. A life-long devotee of good humor and all things sacred and profane, his recent editorial credits include: Travelers' Tales China, The Best Travelers' Tales 2006, Hyenas Laughed at Me and Now I Know Why, Travelers' Tales American Southwest, Travelers' Tales Greece, Travelers' Tales Ireland, Travelers' Tales Grand Canyon, Danger!, Pilgrimage, The Ultimate Journey, Testosterone Planet *and* Stories to Live By. *Widely traveled, Sean most recently completed a journey through the islands of the South Pacific and Malaysia. He lives in Virginia with his wife and six children.*

KYLE KEYSER

Love in a Black Jeep Wrangler

Livin' it up when the pants are down.

WE JUST EXITED HIGHWAY 31 IN MAUI, AND WE'RE PARKED at a shopping center, located at the crossroad of what he wants to do and what I want to do. It's after sunset and we're in a rented, black Jeep Wrangler with a dome light that never goes out. My partner, Adam, is struggling. He doesn't want to drop his shorts.

"I don't know, Kyle," he says, assessing the well-lit parking lot. "Do you think anyone will see?"

This isn't a ploy. He's genuinely shy and has a hypochondriac's sensitivity to people looking at his junk. Still, I'm ready to go. It's a two-hour drive to the chilly summit of Haleakala, and a sky full of stars awaits me. Pants are certainly a requisite. I understand he'd prefer an evening walk on the beach. But relationships are a compromise, you know?

"I'm sure it'll be fine, Adam. I mean, really, who cares?"

He tentatively tugs at the tie of his waistband. I know it isn't helping that he's not the underwear type. Neither of us is; I'm just less concerned about it.

"You know you'll be miserable if you're wearing shorts. It's *really* cold up there."

"I know. But the beach is warmer," he says with side eye and a smile.

I'm pushing him a little and I know it. Haleakala is long dormant but even if it were the towering inferno that originally birthed this island, Adam wouldn't necessarily be the one running up to explore its hills. Nor would he think it's a particularly good idea if you did. But with a little coaxing, he'd follow (and love it). If you extended your hand, he'd probably even join you at the caldera's edge. He'd complain that the heat was singeing his nose hairs but he'd meet you at that edge. And he'd damn sure be wearing pants.

Me, I want a night sky inflated so big it might pop. I want a million shining opportunities to share my knowledge of the cosmos and connect stars to constellations that may or may not really exist. We had a solid day on Earth. Let's go dream at the heavens. It's not often a cloudless night, a moonless sky, and a road 10,000 feet up leads you straight to a place where you can do just that.

"All right, let's do this." I position my thumbs along the sides of my shorts, encouraging him to do the same. "We'll take them off together, on the count of three. No one's watching, I promise."

Adam reluctantly gets into position. I do a quick look-around—the coast is clear— and count, "One, two, three."

A ruffling noise fills the Jeep as we both start slipping off our shorts. I lean into the steering wheel, looking outward as I reach down to pull the trunks from my ankles. Adam takes the lean-back approach, bringing his legs up toward him in order to pull his free. I can't help but chuckle. We take different roads, but we always end up at the same place.

Naked from the waist down, I reach back to grab my pants. Adam has his in hand and starts to slip into them. I steal a glance at the soft whites of his upper thighs while I turn toward the front.

That's when I glimpse someone standing outside my window. I recoil, startled. "What the hell?"

The face looking in is of an older man. He has long, wavy hair with a white streak down the front. His mouth is closed but very noticeably wide. He's just standing there, staring, as if taking in a fine art piece: *Two Naked White Boys, Illuminated in Dome.*

Adam shouts, "Oh my god! Kyle!"

The man continues to stare blankly into the window. His face, on stark display under the high beam of a parking lot light, has deep lines, yet the skin around his eyes is taught. Is this guy real? No, he's a wax figurine, someone rolled into place. He kind of looks like he belongs in a museum. That's when I recognize him.

"Oh my god," I say, trying to place his name. "That's… that's…" And it comes to me: Steven Tyler, of Aerosmith. Wait. Yes. *Oh my god. It's Steven Tyler.*

Suddenly I'm starstruck and all I can do is return the stare. *Who would have thought? Steven Tyler! What the hell is he doing here? Does he live in Maui? Is he on vacation? Is he on tour? What are the odds of this? I mean, really…Steven Tyler. He's like a hundred years old and has so many famous songs. He's a legend! A true legend!*

A weighty feeling tugs at my right hand, and I realize I'm still holding my pants.

Oh my god, that's really Steven Tyler! Staring at my penis!

Unfazed, I lay my pants over my lap and automatically reach out to roll down the window. I have to say something, anything. This moment is too good.

"Kyle, what are you *doing?*" shrieks Adam. I turn toward him, smelling sunblock and sweat, and see panic crawling down his neck, red as sunburn. It's no match for the frozen grip he has on the passenger side seat.

I attempt a limp save, "It's Steven Tyler. Of Aerosmith. We should say hello."

"Kyle do *not* open that window! You're *embarrassing* me!" Adam's declaration echoes in the sudden stillness. His tone carries an alarm that, in our five years together, I've never heard before. It's an alarm that sounds a wave, a tsunami straight from the Pacific Ocean, that fills the cracks of our history together and crashes against the sides of our Jeep. I'm on a new island now, just the size of us, and he is the only one I see here.

Perhaps I pushed too far. Or I was too careless with my attention. Whatever it was, something unlocked in his history that's bigger than me. I don't understand it and maybe I'm never meant to. But like the experience of negotiating a foreign land, so is my relationship with this person. It's the smile that crosses your face when a local welcomes you to dance with her in an unfamiliar custom. Or the song you sing with gusto, even though the words are Chinese.

Adam is a foreign country, with all the riddle and mystery that it entails. And I am the dutiful, deferential traveler who, in this particular instance, finds himself just slightly off the map and needing to get back home.

I reach up and cover the dome light so he can finish dressing.

After taking a few minutes to get situated, I pull onto the highway and head north. Adam is calm, fumbling with his phone in his lap and obviously thinking about something.

"Honey," I say, contrite. "I have a confession." Adam looks at me, curious. "I don't think Steven Tyler saw us naked. In fact, I don't think he saw us at all."

"What do you mean?"

I explain. As Steven Tyler stood there, under the bright lights of the parking lot, he turned without reaction and entered the car next to ours. Instantly, he pulled down the sun visor, poofed his hair, and scrunched his lips into a mirror. He'd been admiring his own reflection in my driver's side window, not us. "So basically," I continue, "we were watching Steven Tyler watching us while really he was only watching himself."

Adam pauses to consider it.

"And if I can be frank, Adam…dude kinda looked like a lady."

Adam breaks into a laugh. "Kyle, you *did not* just say that." He smiles, shakes his head in mock disapproval, and resettles into his seat. "Well," he says after a minute or two, "you could have opened the window if you wanted. I mean, it *was* Steven Tyler." He throws me a guilty smile and a proverbial hand, one accepting a little more help onto the edge.

Ahead, I see a sign for Haleakala National Park. At the next intersection, the volcano's summit will be 50 miles to the right. The Ka'anapali beaches will be 32 miles to the left.

Adam looks down at his phone. "I need to play a song to mark this occasion."

As the first few *uh-mm-mm-mm-mm-mmmms* of Aerosmith's "Love in an Elevator" ring out, I slow to approach the coming intersection. Adam is focused on his lap, consumed with Aerosmith's discography. He scrolls with one hand and finds mine with the other, grabbing it firmly as I, we, hold the main gearshift. He caresses the top of my hand with his thumb.

My turn signals remain a blank slate in the night sky, and it's not until I'm upon the intersection that I decide to turn left, toward the beach. There will be plenty of stars there, I imagine. The air fills with a sweetness, of pineapples, and long strings of streetlights lead the way to the shore.

Kyle Keyser is a recovering filmmaker, former mayoral candidate, and future something-or-other. To be continued. www.kyle.tv

JILL PARIS

Africa à la Carte

Saved by a frickin' saint!

"Lamu's not that far—it's just a bit north of here," I explained to Lori as if I knew what the hell I was talking about. Up until a month before, I'd never even heard of the secluded island once referred to as "the black hole of laidbackness," thanks to the hippies and artists who'd infiltrated the African hideaway back in the '60s.

"You can't fly off on your own!" she yelled. "It's too dangerous!!"

"Sure I can," I assured her. "Trust me. No one'll even miss me."

At the beginning of our three-week safari throughout Kenya and Tanzania, Lori and I were assigned together as roommates by the travel company on account of our being the youngest out of 30 travelers, not because we were BFFs. I hardly knew her. Jeez, by her reaction you'd have thought I'd renounced my citizenship to stay and live naked amongst baboons or something.

The year was 1987—the decade of big hair and decadence. We'd been schlepping around en masse for weeks and, on that day, our group's activity was to visit an open market then return to Mombasa for yet another buffet feast. Fruit-gazing just doesn't do it for me, in Kenya or anywhere else, so I had decided to break free and see what revelatory powers Lamu had to satisfy my 20-something curiosity. And besides, our strict itinerary reminded me of a prix fixe menu's limitations—for one set price you'll eat what we're serving, when we say, or go hungry. I wanted to order something "off the menu" for a change.

"What should I tell *Hans*?" Lori whispered as if saying his name too loudly might conjure up bad spirits. "He'll forbid you to go."

Hans happened to be our stern Danish tour guide, who I'm pretty sure hoped I'd catch Dengue fever and die. Everyone on the tour couldn't have been nicer, and I certainly meant no disrespect by my need to exclude myself at any opportunity, but I think Hans kind of hated me for being the "antijoiner." I sensed his loathing after I'd snuck off during a bathroom break at Chania Falls when the game drives first began. He'd glanced down at his watch, then back at me with real condemnation (probably because I'd smoked a cigarette and downed a Tusker beer before breakfast). After that incident, he'd "accidentally" omit me from the day's rotating seat assignment. I'd often end up bouncing around in the back of the bus, where the seat's worn-out springs had sprung to epic recoil. It was nauseating. Lori nicknamed it "the trampoline."

"Just tell him…whatever! Who knows? Maybe I'll disappear," I joked. "He'll probably be thrilled."

Lori shook her head, seemingly displeased by my decision to a) ditch the group without clearing it with our leader, and b) jet off unaccompanied to a teeny, smidge of an island without cars. But, most baffling of all to her was probably why in the hell I was outfitted as a cast member from the award-winning film *Out of Africa*? I'll admit the captivating flick not only inspired me to visit Isak

Dinesen's real home outside of Nairobi and dream of becoming a writer, but the movie's period costumes must have prompted some sort of bullshit pretense in me to try and look the part of the author as well. So, yes, if you squinted hard enough, I might have passed as Baroness Blixen's shoddy relation in a white muslin maxi dress I'd mail-ordered through Banana Republic back when the store's garments were designed for off-the-beaten-path adventurers with its cool catalogue filled with treasure maps, steamer trunks, and an abundance of khaki and canvas. Upon my head sat a straw boater hat I'd recently purchased in London to complete the impersonation. My answer to the unflattering pith helmet, I guess.

The hotel concierge in Mombasa arranged for my flight and a private tour guide to escort me around Lamu on foot (as the only method of transportation there was either bicycle or beast). Also included in the day trip was "a leisurely lunch at a seaside restaurant and an afternoon cruise on an authentic dhow." I wasn't sure what that meant but didn't really care, as the low-key, do-as-I-damn-well-please excursion sounded like bliss on a stick.

I stared at the non-English-speaking pilot, who motioned for me to sit beside him in a plane so tiny the instrument panel compared to that of a midsize automobile's interior. Seriously, it was like a Toyota with wings. Then, three male French backpackers arrived and tucked themselves in like folding chaises. The grungy trio did not take their seats (because there weren't any) and instead crouched down on the cabin floor exposing their tanned legs for my viewing pleasure, plus the bonus lack of boxers or briefs under their shorts. *Bonjour, Messieurs.*

In no time, the plane touched down on the isle of Manda, and soon we were directed onto a small boat made out of kindling. The lithe skipper huffed and puffed while steering his oars through jerky waters to the brink of an asthmatic attack. I'm not sure which was worse, the sight of the cutest dude's failure to conceal his seasickness, or the amount of ass-splinters I accrued from the vessel's fine attempt to capsize. In this case, it was a toss up.

Once we finally reached Lamu, a bastardly breeze snatched that bonnet right off my head, and I watched part of my new persona haul ass down a dirt road, as if being chased by wild dogs. Deeply saddened over the loss (and now sporting major hat hair), I followed about 50 yards behind the others, when, out of the wistful air, an unusual voice called out.

"You must be my client because...I found your hat," said a podgy man in baggy, black trousers that were about six inches too long for him. He clutched the brim with childlike pride, shifting his weight from side to side, then sort of bowed before me with his arms extended.

"Oh, thank you!" I shouted. "Thank you so much."

"I am Mohammed," he said with a thin smile. "Come. Please."

I learned quickly that he was born "somewhere in the middle of nine children." His eyes were as dark as espresso with weathered skin to match. What a pair we must have been, lily-white me towering at least a foot over him, shrouded in the hopeful disguise to be somebody else, and he in what very well may have been another man's clothes as well.

Mohammed led me to a majestic structure where scads of chanting men, each one kneeling and bowing like mad, crooned verses in a strange language. I'd never seen a mosque in person before or ever visited a place where kicking one's shoes off and pressing one's forehead to the ground was the official way to pray. It felt wrong to be penetrating their sacred space—forbidden. Kind of like the time in high school when all the cheerleaders inadvertently broke into the wrong house while we were "kidnapping" one of the football players who, unbeknownst to us, lived on the next street. It's a wonder we weren't jailed for breaking and entering, but it's kind of nice to know if I ever need to jimmy a lock somewhere I totally have a knack for that shit.

Mohammed tapped me on the shoulder and shifted his eyes sideways as a signal to leave. We ducked out quietly with the hum of gratefulness lingering long after we'd gone.

Some chickens pecking at the same stupid pebbles blocked our path to a narrow alley surrounded by high stony walls, but luckily a man leading a donkey with fruit piled at an insane tilt angered the birds into a scatter.

"Would you like to buy a *khanga?*" Mohammed inquired.

"Sure," I replied, thinking it might be some kind of illegal pet worth smuggling home.

"This way," he said, guiding me down a slanted passageway so slim, I could practically hold my arms out and touch both sides.

The stones' hue shone like pink tourmaline even in the shade. There weren't any written signs above, below, or in between the surrounding rock. I didn't notice any numbered markings or addresses either. I thought maybe he had to tally his paces to find his way around, like a blind person does. Just in case, I remained super quiet so he wouldn't lose count.

Just inside an open doorway, long tables housing stacks of fabrics in every color combination soon clarified that a "*khanga*" was in no way against the law but was actually a sarong garment made of cotton, worn mostly by ladies and even some men.

"They're all so beautiful. Which one do you like?" I asked my trusty guide, but before he could answer, an ear-piercing "OH, MY GAWD!" startled us both. There she stood, the loud, bushy-haired woman who one month ago had complimented the Irish linen dress I was wearing as we strolled through Heathrow Airport to catch our respective flights. She had five or six pieces of cloth draped over each arm. Her frizzy 'do had been swept up with frayed raffia, but it totally worked on her. She reminded me of a rich, New York fashion designer who only parties on yachts and collects vintage sunglasses just for the hell of it.

"Oh, my Gaaaawd!! What are the chances!?" she kept saying over and over like a mantra. Yeah, what *were* the odds that I'd bump into someone familiar on a miniscule island off the coast of Kenya in a back room of an unmarked *khanga* shop that had taken a dinky plane, a rickety boat, and a maze of masonry to reach? About 800 billion to 1? Lamu was kind of freaking me out.

I glanced over at Mohammed to see if he was as stunned as I by the mysterious fluke. Perhaps he didn't get how molecularly random it was because he didn't really seem all that surprised.

I sorted through the vibrant materials in an effort to choose the best pattern, but the woman pushed in and said, "You should have this one" and handed me an indigo and sea-green tinted design. "I'll even get it for you." And, before I could refuse, she paid the vendor and was out the door in a rush to meet her husband back at the Peponi Hotel, a favorite retreat amongst British celebs, royals, and the like.

Before long, Mohammed and I approached what looked like someone's humble abode that faced the whitest beach with sand the color of crushed pearls. I thought maybe he'd brought me home to meet his family, and any second his much-taller brother would burst out half-nude and demand Mohammed return his only pair of trousers.

As we drew closer, the smoky scent of grilled cuisine overtook me, and I discovered a kick-ass brawl was probably not going to happen.

"This is where I leave you," he said. "I will be back in one and half hours."

I watched him disappear down the lane and missed him as soon as he'd vanished.

I took a seat next to a fortyish woman dining alone (the only other patron), and she introduced herself as "Mmmonika the Mmmissionary" with inflated alliteration the way a schoolteacher does unwittingly. Her German accent was as thick as the thatched roof above the outdoor eating area. I'd never met a working nun before, or even seen one in plain clothes. It made me a little nervous to think how she'd judge me if I confessed to blowing off my tour group without telling the man in charge and had come here to Lamu on a "wild hair" (one of my mother's sayings when I do stupid things), all because a radio disc jockey named John Logic that I liked back home said I simply *had* to check out Lamu no matter what. Maybe Monika would phone the authorities and turn me in? Or better yet, have my disobedient ass flogged right over there next to that snoozing fisherman. But I said nothing.

She and I gazed out across Lamu Bay in quiet contemplation like two scholars set to observe a slide show presentation on "How to Properly Observe the World's Beauty in Complete and Utter Silence."

"How would you pronounce that color in English, please?" Monika asked pointing at the horizon.

"I'm not really sure," I replied. "Cornflower?" But I knew that wasn't right. It may have been closer to cerulean or somewhere in the dusky-powder family.

"I have never seen a sky so blue," Monika said in awe.

"Neither have I."

I swear if there's an Admirals Lounge in the afterlife for Cosmic Travelers, I'll bet its walls are painted that celestial shade of Lamu blue. I'll have to remember to check it out when I get there.

While I pondered which was prettier, the actual sky or its reflection spread over the satiny sea, a giant plate of fresh-caught lobster and drawn butter was placed before me. I cracked open the shell and bit into the steaming white meat, golden liquid oozing down my wrists, as Monika shared the details of her virtuous life working with a foreign aid organization. Together we marveled over a few new shades of rose, violet, and gray we swore had never been glimpsed either by anyone alive or dead.

In time, Mohammed reappeared, so I bid farewell to my pious friend and followed him down a winding trail onto an empty cove, where two African sailors with broad smiles welcomed me aboard their dhow. It looked like something the Owl and the Pussycat went to sea in. Secured to the top of the mast were sprigs of bougainvillea, sort of like the floral cherry atop a slivered sundae.

Once I climbed aboard, the men prepared to push off and, after several minutes of sitting calmly and waiting for enough wind to raise the triangular sail to carry us away, we were moving. Coasting at a dawdling speed, the lovely view of Lamu from that distance reminded me of a scene inside a snow globe. Its beauty protected beneath an invisible dome, peaceful and untouched, until something comes along, breaks it wide-open, and all of its contents spill out.

Was it the humidity of the July heat, the aroma of the town, or the scent of the tropics that made Lamu unique? Was it the brilliance of the midday sky crying out for a nap, or the glare of the whitewashed stone houses, the strong winds blowing off the ocean rustling the *makuti* roofs that looked so enchanting? Or maybe it was the

Portugese cannons perfectly aligned on the waterfront, the absence of automobiles, or the narrowness of the streets, the romantic architecture of galleries and harem rooms of the Patrician Stone Houses that all came together in splendiferous precision. I thought to myself, "John Logic, you are going to get sooo lucky when I get home."

One of the men began to sing aloud, his chaste voice wrestling against the wind but thankfully winning out for my private concert.

"What is that?" I asked. My God, the haunting tune brought tears to my eyes.

"It's a love song from Zanzibar," he said.

I knew I wouldn't be able to remember the melody and certainly none of the Swahili lyrics, but at that moment it became the song of my life, the song I'd traveled so far to hear. Its significance moved me. Jeez, no wonder hippies flocked here in droves.

Suddenly, my body lurched forward and ricocheted against the bottom with a thud. My satchel and precious *khanga* also went flying off the seat, as the captain, clinging to the mast pole, turned and laughingly stated, "Please, do not worry. All will be well."

The boat had stopped moving, which seemed altogether surreal. I looked back and saw yards of rippling foam had left white skid marks behind us.

For the crew, this was business as usual, but for me, a freak sandbar incident was not funny or in any way part of the package. My plane was set to leave in less than an hour, and the windless launch had already postponed the timeframe allotted for my cruise. We were far from shore, and the only other dhows we'd passed were long out of sight.

While watching the guys, for what seemed like days, try to free the boat, I remembered this little game in elementary school I loved to play, where I'd spin the globe on my teacher's desk and stop the turning sphere abruptly with my index finger and declare, "THIS is where I am going to end up someday." Of course nine out of ten times I'd land smack in the middle of the "blue part" and demand a do-over in hopes of landing on a cool "green part." This was kind of like that, only there wasn't a plastic orb handy for one more whirl. No, it was just me and a couple of African dudes in loin-cloths stranded somewhere south of the equator—ship-wrecked—alone on the Indian Ocean.

I reckoned this was some kind of payback for my bratty behavior. If only I'd told Hans where I was going, then maybe I wouldn't be in a situation where I was about to be "knocked upside the head" which is yet another one of my mother's charming sayings.

The men jumped over the side and swam toward the islet. With all their might, they grabbed onto the outer hull whilst fighting the surf, and kicked their feet. Still, the craft would not budge.

"Can you help us?" the commander pleaded.

Just as I stood up, ready to jump ship and plunge fully clothed into the depths of the ocean deep, the dhow released itself and began to drift backwards. Both men heaved their lean bodies up and over the side of the boat like trained seals.

By the time we reached Lamu, I spied poor Mohammed sitting by the docks awaiting my return. He'd arranged for me to take a different flight, but mentioned I'd arrive later than expected. What a relief, I thought, as the tour was leaving for Samburu the next morning, and if I missed that, then I'd really be in trouble.

Now back on Manda, I signed the guestbook near the runway, a registry of thoughts from people who'd vis-ited Lamu Island over the years. I scribbled "I hope to come back again someday with someone I love." I kind of felt guilty for not sharing the day and found myself kind of missing Lori and her worrisome ways, the chatter of the ladies at dinner time, and even their lively discussions about teacher strikes, who did or didn't get tenure, or really important issues like how rough the toilet paper had been on safari.

Once inside the larger airplane, I spotted Mmmonika in the back left seat reading quietly, looking rather angelic. I settled in across from her, the only other seat onboard. This plane seemed wider, better. Maybe it was for the best I'd been delayed. No copiloting duties for me this return.

A man hopped in and prepared the engines for takeoff. I was half hoping to turn around and see those French boys sitting cross-legged behind me, nuts and all, but it was just us three.

I regaled Monika with my tale aboard the stubborn dhow that wouldn't move, and then, after we'd reached cruising altitude, that hideous, undeniable symptom usually associated with acute drunks or amoebic dysentery hit. The unmistakable "clear the decks, I'm going to puke-my-sandals-up-through-my-intestines" urge that rammed me faster than that dhow had come to a halt. Oh, the salivating sensation behind the molars that invades your mouth, like tarantulas on your tongue. My forehead suddenly felt hosed down with perspiration. I'm guessing my skin was as white as my dress because I was losing consciousness fast.

My stomach twerked back and forth like it was trying to churn butter or something. Oh man, I'll bet it was the BUTTER! That slick, yellow, mother effing bowl of butter I'd been served at lunch and used to sop up what seemed like a seven-pound crustacean as though it was my last meal—ever.

Then, for some reason, I pictured that infamous scene in the movie *Stand By Me* when Gordy tells his buddies a campfire story he'd written about a kid named Davey Hogan, who drinks a bottle of castor oil before a pie-eating contest (a retribution plot for all the evil jerks who'd called him Lard-Ass for being overweight), and after gorging himself on blueberry pies during the festivities, a thunderous noise like a runaway log truck alerts the audience that some major shit is about to go down. Once he blows chunks, the smell overtakes the crowd, and every single participant and spectator barfs, too, and soon all are covered in slimy, purple spewage for the ultimate revenge, or as Gordy puts it, "a complete and total Barf-O-Rama."

What if after losing my lunch in here the pilot passes out from the stench? Who'll fly the plane? I may kill us all! I was skating on thin tailspin territory here.

I turned toward Monika and with one lethal glance she could tell what was about to happen. She quickly rummaged through her sack then whipped out a clear plastic baggie and gave it to me. It was a miracle only a wise woman of the cloth could perform so selflessly. But have you ever had to carry a see-through bag of your own vomit for several minutes whilst airborne inside a turbulent plane? It ain't easy.

Monika stared out the window in silence, hopefully praying for my absolution. I sort of lay there melded into the seat, dazed, still weak from the release, in emptied, gutted shock.

The pilot must have heard the guttural upchuck and turned back in time to catch me holding the bag like I'd won the prize goldfish at a school fair, with bits of turgid flesh morbidly visible, still warm to the touch.

After what seemed like ten years had passed, we finally arrived at the Mombasa airstrip upon blessed, flat land. I was just thankful a SWAT team with guns wasn't there to arrest me (though I probably deserved to be shot).

Monika left the plane first. I couldn't imagine what was going through her mind. How did she know to pack an airsick bag? What a frickin' saint!

As I stepped out onto the folding ladder, embarrassed, yet oddly elegant in my Karen Blixen get-up, the pilot kindly took hold of my carry-on "saggage," walked about 50 yards in front of the plane's propeller, and tossed my leisurely lunch onto the tarmac.

I prepared myself for whatever penance Hans had in store for me. After that sickening flight, "the trampoline" would be a piece of cake. And, no sooner than I could adjust my hat to its rightful position, a flock of seagulls swooped down and began feasting on my "just desserts" as if they'd been expecting it.

★

Jill Paris is the author of Life is Like a Walking Safari. *Her essays have been published in the Travelers' Tales anthologies* The Best Travel Writing 2009, Leave the Lipstick, Take the Iguana *and* The Best Women's Travel Writing Volume 9. *Other essays have also been featured in* The Saturday Evening Post, Travel Africa, Gadling, Thought Catalog, *and more. She travels for the inexplicable human connection.*

Postcard from Kenya

"You never know what worse luck your bad luck has saved you from."
—*Cormac McCarthy,* No Country for Old Men

THERE COMES A MOMENT IN EVERY MAN'S LIFE WHEN HE FINDS himself on his knees, shoveling up his own shit with his ever-blackening bare hands, while an angry family of strangers screams invectives at him in a language he does not understand. The hope in such moments is to escape with dignity. I was on the road from Laisamis when such tribulations befell me.

Laisamis is in the Kenyan north, a region to which the Western world, in its inexorable onward march, has still only sent advance sentries. The Kenyan police get progressively more unpleasant as you move farther north (ostensibly, this is because shit's realer up there) and today they are in standard form, berating a Pakistani man in a tight-fitting black-and-orange cycling jersey. Some rummage through his belongings, occasionally pausing to further inspect a sock. Others question him directly, occasionally pausing midsentence to let some of the green *miraa* they've been chewing fall from their mouths onto the piles at their feet. It reminds me of when an elephant takes a shit. They are all sunglasses and camouflage and testosterone. They motion their guns menacingly.

Simon and I need to catch the day's final charter to Nairobi (we'll be getting off in Nanyuki), and it is imperative that we obtain tickets before it leaves this hot and dusty place. I am personally shadowed by a haggle of elderly Rendile women who wish to sell me their jewelry, but Simon, who is Kenyan, remains focused on the task at hand.

The driver sees that Simon is with me—I am wearing a tan bucket hat that says *Ranger Rick* on it, if that gives any indication of my skin color—and doubles the price. I tell Simon that I'll just pay it, but privy to local sales practices, Simon is not so easily had. I can't understand it, but I imagine he says the Swahili equivalent of "*Naw*, I don't pay that shit." The driver nods.

"While you're with me in Kenya, there is no need to worry," says Simon with that bouncy Kenyan cadence that is somehow all at once innocent and wise. "You will always be fine." The bus is nearly full. Eyes of our fellow passengers track us as we walk down the aisle. Outside, the jewel saleswomen push up against the bus windows. The sale is slipping away, and they are slashing prices like mad.

Simon and I sit down in the back next to a 13-year-old boy named Patrick. I look out the window. The Pakistani man is arguing with the same soldier who had spent three minutes mistrustfully panning his face back and forth between me and my ID the previous day. The engine rumbles to life. The Pakistani man grabs his belongings and bounds aboard. Away we go.

The road from Laisamis is not paved. Indeed, it is not paved in the Kenyan sense, meaning that it is borderline impassable without four-wheel drive. Our driver does not take this into account when calculating his velocity. Almost in rhythm, every five seconds, a powerful jolt launches the passengers up and out of their seats in an elegant synchrony. Unfazed, everyone maintains a blank forward stare. Patrick and I giggle hysterically in the back. The road from Laisamis meanders through a brown, hard desert interspersed with small acacia bushes and windowless shacks, whose chief structural components are newspaper and dried cow dung. Occasionally, we pass a shirtless citizen wrapped in a red kilt and colorful bead accessories, herding his cows and camels. I chat with Patrick, who explains that he is on the way to Nairobi to begin secondary school. "*Ninajifunza Kiswahili*"—I am learning Swahili—I tell him, and he tells me the words for chair and window.

The pavement begins, and with it a series of police stops. The ritual is always the same. Angry guy in uniform snarls at me and the fact that I only have my ID and no passport, then growls at a few other people, and then pulls the Pakistani guy off the bus to see his bag. Onward ho. At one police stop there are men in dress shirts and neckties. They hold rifles. The bus driver grabs a briefcase and gets off the bus. I look around, all eyes are focused out the right window toward the three men. I ask Patrick what is going on. "We cannot go farther," he says.

I blink. "What?"

No response. We watch the driver approach the men. They talk for some minutes. Lots of gesticulation. Silence in the bus. The driver hands the case to the tallest man with the smallest rifle. I look at Patrick. He smiles. "They accepted," he whispers.

Roadside charcoal vendors tie up their bags. Uniformed school children cheerfully waddle the final stretch of their journey home. Orange clouds, distant hills, and small aca-cia cast long shadows upon the plains of Samburu County.

Day turns to night in Kenya.

We are ten minutes short of Isiolo, an hour from Nanyuki, when a stout policewoman with tight short braids below her cap steps onto the bus. I relax. No testos-terone-fueled power trip to worry about here. She comes to me first, holds out her hand. I nudge up toward Patrick like always, smile a winner, and nod as I give her my ID.

She frowns. Where is my passport? I explain that I'd been warned against bringing my passport on account of the dangerous roads. Then she turns around and walks away without handing back the ID. I look at Patrick. He shrugs. I look at Simon. He shrugs.

"Excuse me," I say to the woman, but Simon holds me back. It's not worth it.

She takes a few more passports, and then grabs a few more still. A woman in a hijab says that she has no right to do this. The officer ignores her. Those who have had their passports taken disembark in outrage. I tell Simon the ID replacement fee is "probably like $300." Simon agrees this is *worth* fighting for. We file off last, leaving our belongings in Patrick's charge.

Motorbike silhouettes zip and zoom through the night. The policewoman sits in a roadside shack with an authori-tative chubby-faced man who gets a masculine thrill out of shining his jumbo flashlight directly into the eyes of those he questions.

Initially there is a crowd, but slowly, fifteen turns to five, then to three, then, once all have retrieved their pass-ports—it's just me, Simon, and the police. The language jumps between Kikuyu, Swahili, and English. I catch flashes. They want money. No they don't. No they do, they want 5,000 shillings—about $60 U.S. "*Hapana,*" says

Simon (we have no money). I'm a *mzungu* (white man), so the assumption is, I have money.

"Fine, 1,000 shillings," says the woman.

"*Hapana!*"

The bus rumbles.

"Five hundred."

It moves.

"Four hundred."

It drives away. Our possessions are still on board.

The cop shines his light in my eyes and sees the dismay. "Don't worry, it'll stop in Isiolo for a bit. How about 300?"

Simon doesn't let up. It's standard to pay bribes in Kenya (though less and less so) but I get the sense that Simon's determination is fueled by a sense of national pride in front of a visitor. The police eventually get the message and unapologetically hand back the ID. They tell us to scram, and Simon and I storm off down the unlit roadside.

Bodaboda shadows continue to whiz by. Simon whistles. One of the motorcycles pulls over. No words are exchanged. The two of us hop on. "Isiolo," says Simon.

The air is cool on my face. I am in the center, the driver in front and Simon hanging on behind. We weave around a sand truck and a car weaves around us. Some motorbikes have no lights. You hear them. You don't see them.

Then it begins with the first speed bump—a stirring in the guts. A pothole: the bowels grumble. And then zero to a hundred in ten seconds. It's a code blue.

The faraway glow of Isiolo turns bright and immediate. Buses line the road. Which is ours? Has it left? I haven't yet told Simon of my impending emergency. Beads of sweat condense on my lower back. The motorcycle zooms onward.

All at once there's pain and numbness in my nethers. The internal sphincter has fallen. The external sphincter weakens. Adrenaline shoots from my kidneys. *There's the bus! No, wrong one! No, it's that one over there!* We motor. Bump, bump, bump. What kind of bullshit shocks are these? Then we see Patrick's round bucktoothed face jammed out a bus window. He waves. Simon waves back. I can't wave. It's a blur. We get off the motorbike. I tell Simon about my problem. He asks the bus driver where I can go. Driver says, "No time."

We climb the stairs. All the passengers are staring and smiling. The *mzungu* made it back! A guy who speaks American English starts telling me about his week in North Dakota. I nod. My face is red. We head to the back. Patrick pats the seat he saved for me and I ignore him. I sit alone in the row in front of him and press my head against the window.

It's 50 minutes to Nanyuki. This thought zaps my aching sphincter of its remaining strength. Simon sees me.

"What's wrong?" asks Patrick. I glare at him. Poor Patrick. He could never understand. Simon and I lock eyes. *He* understands. The gate cannot hold.

"One minute," yells Simon to the driver as we hightail off the bus. The driver, who is leaning on the bus's side, does not respond. Simon and I zigzag through the throngs. *"Choo iko wapi? Choo iko wapi?!"* Simon and I collide. Our heads turn. We see it together. A clinic!

Inside, my eyes scan. Where, where, where??? I spin. I see something that says lavatory and I desperately shake the door handle.

"That's the *laboratory*," yells Simon.

Patrons of the clinic watch. I dance a frantic high-step jig and they gape in silence. I lock eyes with Simon again, and he is pointing towards the open back door.

Yes, there it is—a beacon in the night. A corrugated metal shed housing a pit latrine. I make a bowlegged dash. Sweet relief is on the way. I pull the door. It's locked.

"I'll find a key," Simon shouts, and he runs back inside.

The air is humid. I lean on the side of the shed and drag myself around it. Movement is essential. Hold, sphincter, hold! There is a field of grass. It is dark. A mosque rises above the wood shacks that surround the field. It is illuminated and ostentatious. Its crisp clean spires rise towards the black heavens. The cars and voices of the city beyond the clinic are barely audible. I look to the sky. Bubbles below. There is no strength remaining. Simon has not returned in time. The bus will soon leave. All is lost. There is no hope. I can hold no more.

The lights of the mosque cast deep shadows on the grass. They flicker and shake. Holy crap, it's everywhere. *Everywhere.* "Simon," I groan. "I…I didn't make it." Simon, who had obtained the key, sees my predicament and sprints back inside. It is me and the wind.

I look around and take inventory of the situation: my pants cast off a couple feet to my right—my boxers inside them. I have my favorite tan polo on top and nothing on my bottom. I crawl over to my trousers and dig through the pockets to get my phone and wallet and keys. It's tricky. There is much to avoid. I hear a sound. I look up.

A woman in a hijab stands five feet away. We make eye contact and both freeze. A couple seconds go by.

It's unclear how long she has been standing here but it *doesn't* take long to deduce that this is her yard. In calculating my next move, I consider the situation as she must see it. To her, I am a naked cursing white man crawling in and around his own shit just outside of a perfectly suitable bathroom. She sees a pale white ass gleaming in the darkness and smells a damp combo of fecal matter and Old Spice deodorant—*If your grandpa hadn't worn it, you wouldn't be alive!*

I defer the first move to the woman. A few more seconds of silence, and then she makes her play, a high-pitched and extended shriek, "AAHAAAAHHAWAAR! AAAWWTTSAAAA!"

I stand, exposing a horrifying segment more of my pale frame. The shriek morphs into words but they are not in English.

"Sorry sorry sorry sorry sorry sorry sorry sorry," I sputter, throwing myself into a crouch.

She doesn't let up.

Her little girls come out, all in hijabs. They cover their mouths and giggle. The woman continues to scream

I cover myself. "It was an *accident*! Can't you see!?"

A horn honks on the other side of the clinic. There goes the bus. There go all of my belongings, again. The screaming continues. Another woman comes out and adds her screams. Outnumbered, I retreat into my own head and think of a time, weeks in the future, when (unless I get deported) this will be an amusing memory.

Simon rounds the latrine in a full sprint. He has his bag. He has *my* bag.

He evaluates the situation and dives into his backpack for some jeans. "Put these on!" He hurls them my way. I wrestle into them. The waistband is huge. It slips down around my ass but, still, one dignity is reclaimed.

Simon assumes a power stance directly between the woman and me. He speaks a calm confident Swahili. I cower behind him. I don't want to make eye contact with anybody so I stare at the ground, but then I have to look at the shit that is between my feet because in my terror it didn't occur to me to move. I have a firm grip on each side of the jeans. Now a girl, maybe fifteen, emerges from the house. She looks at the ground around me, then at my skin, then places her hand on her hips.

"Hey! Where you from?" she demands in English. She pops her hips to the left.

I don't respond.

"Hey! I'm talkin' to you. Where are you from?"

"The U.S.," I mumble. I can't just ignore her. I did, after all, just take a shit in her yard.

"Is this what you do in America? Huh? You just go around and *feces* in other people's yard?"

I stare blankly at her. The scent of digested goat-*ugali*-bean-banana begins to waft outward. Simon and the mother continue to do battle in Swahili on the side.

"Huh? Is that what you do over there? Well, welcome to Africa, welcome to Kenya, *we don't do that here.*" She is quite pleased with herself. She's doing that thing with her hand where you twist your wrist in a circle, and then thrust the hand out towards the victim, palm first. She does that repeatedly. Her other hand, the left one, still rests on her hip.

I try to explain that in fact we don't *feces* in other people's yards in America, that this was an honest mistake, that I'm on a trip to visit some motherfucking *kids* we *sponsor* to go to *school,* thank you very much, but I only get about five words in before Simon turns and glares and warns me not to speak to her.

The father comes out. "*Mzungu!*" he booms. "Sit. Down!"

I obey, terrified.

"Don't sit down," yells Simon. "Do. Not. Sit. Down!"

"*MZUNGU!* SIT, DOWN!" yells the man again. He has positioned himself opposite to me.

"NO!" yells Simon. I'm in a partial squat. I maintain a firm grip on the sides of my pants.

The dad demands a thorough cleaning of the entire impact zone. Simon scrambles to find a receptacle and I just half stand there, mute, surrounded. After an eternity, Simon returns from the clinic with a yellow plastic grocery bag. He throws it to me. On knees, I begin with the pants and the underwear. The belt is still salvageable, but there is no time. Christ, this smells bad. All of it goes in the bag. Then it's on to the real stuff, no denim to shield my hand this time. I hold my breath and go for it: grab, throw, grab, throw. The rabble around me is furious. It is not clean enough.

The father aggressively shakes his head. He bellows something at Simon, and Simon runs off and brings back a stick. "I'll dig, you shovel," he says, and he repeatedly jabs his stick into the impact zone. I scrape up the stick's end products with my now-black right hand and toss everything into the bag. Stab, dig, stab, dig. I'm ripping up grass. No remains.

The shouting hasn't abated. "What about there?!" yells the English-speaking girl. "*Hapa. Hapa. HAPA!*"

It's all in the bag. Lights flicker from the mosque. I can hear my heart beat.

Curious onlookers materialize out of the darkness. Now there are a dozen more spectators. Simon explains and explains. I keep hearing the world "*polezi.*" I keep hearing big numbers followed by "*shilingi.*" The 15-year-old continues to spit sassy vitriol. She keeps using "feces" as a verb. This irks me.

Her anger turns to Simon. "This is the man you choose to be your role model in Kenya? *Him?*" She looks disgusted. "Maybe you should make better choices about who you hang around with, don't you think?"

Simon remains stoic. He appears to be making progress in his negotiation. The conversation becomes more subdued. No longer will they call the police. Then no longer do they want money. Mostly now they just want me out of their sight. The breakthrough, I learned, resulted from the culturally prominent tribal structure of Kenya. They were speaking Kikuyu amongst themselves, and Simon responded in kind. They could work with him.

Simon turns around. "Let's go."

I follow without saying a word. I hear the voice—that goddamn girl's voice behind me. "What? You're not even gonna say *thank* you? That's *real* polite."

I mumble a "thank you" and trudge behind Simon into the clinic. Everyone inside knows. Everyone stares. The bloated yellow bag swings in the grip of my black, crusted hand.

The town is dead except for the glue fiends and the corn salesmen. We walk in silence at the side of the road. Cats and rats dig through garbage. We walk. What am I going to do with my bag? What are *we* going to do?

"Simon," I mumble, "I don't, I don't really know what to say. I owe you *so* many Tuskers. I'm sorr—"

"You owe me nothing. It was an accident. You are my brother."

We walk in silence some more.

"Simon, why didn't you want me to sit down?"

"Why should you sit down? You did nothing wrong. Why should you be shamed like that?"

There are a good many reasons why I ought to have been shamed like that, but I just nod and smile. At this point I have known Simon for around ten days. He's been wonderful to me. I have done nothing in return. I may have bought him a few Tuskers here and there to even the score, but already the scales were *so* tipped in his favor. It's the sort of generosity for which forward payment, as opposed to individual repayment, is required.

We decide the best thing to do is just to find some way to get home, back to Nanyuki, back to Wama, back to a place we know. Simon spots a private *matatu* across the street.

The minibus driver, a man with a flat cap, a cigarette, and a black leather jacket, nods at us.

His voice is a Freeman-esque legato. "There's a shower in that hotel over there. I'll wait outside."

The hotel owner sees me and the bag. He understands. He directs me to a corrugated metal shack, not unlike the pit latrine. I enter dirty. I emerge clean.

The owner laughs. "*Karibu* Isiolo," he yells happily as Simon and I walk away into the night. "You're welcome back any time."

The cab is waiting outside. Simon goes to find some gin, and I take a seat on the right hand side behind the driver. He strikes a match and the interior of the *matatu* glows orange. His silhouette deepens. Distant mad cries outside heighten the empty silence inside. He lights his cigarette, takes a drag, and then cigarette in hand, rests his right arm on the open windowsill. He exhales. His breath is slow and deep and thoughtful.

"My friend," he asks, "where did it all go wrong?"

★

Andrew Schwartz recently worked for a small CBO in Kenya during his gap year. His writing experience consists of such works as "In-N-Out Burger and the American Dream" and "Fear and Loathing in Suquamish" for his high school newspaper.

I Had a Passion for the Christ

She wasn't a Jesus freak until she freaked for Jesus.

As 50 other tourists and I entered the cave, a man dressed in a pharaoh's outfit handed us each a cracker and a teeny-tiny wooden cup of grape juice, which looked like a shot glass from biblical times. It was The Last Supper and we'd be breaking bread with Jesus himself in T-minus five minutes.

I wasn't Christian and I didn't believe in Jesus anymore, but I thought it might be kind of fun to visit the Christian-themed amusement park in Orlando, Florida. One of my favorite things to do is immerse myself in a culture that I usually make fun of in order to understand it better. I figured spending the day with Bible thumpers at a Jesus amusement park might help me see religious folks in a new light.

After exploring Noah's Ark, which had nothing but a cardboard cut-out of Jesus and an arcade game, I took a stroll through a giant plastic purple whale, where I found my man, Jonah, floating around. I tried to show off my vocals at "Celebrate Jesus Karaoke," but people didn't respond well to my performance of the only non-gospel tune in the book, "I Believe I Can Fly." I even endured a frighteningly patriotic show, the only one at Holy Land not based on a Bible story, called "The God Bless America Show," and applauded along with the crowd as the man in uniform on stage proudly announced he didn't mind being crippled for the rest of his life because getting shot in war was God's will for him.

At first it felt disrespectful being a non-believer among all these good Christian men and women, like a Russian spy wandering around the Pentagon. But then it occurred to me I'd always felt this way. Even as a kid I thought Jesus was a load of crap. Sure, I'd attended Sunday school, prayed a lot, and sung in the church choir through my sophomore year in high school, but only to make my mom happy.

As soon as I hit sixteen, though, I decided to do what I darn well pleased, mostly drugs. While all my peers spent Sunday mornings studying the Bible in church, I was always hot-boxing a joint in the parking lot or rummaging through the church kitchen with a bad case of the munchies. My mom finally dropped her good-Christian-daughter agenda after I was busted drinking and smoking on a choir tour and sent home in a van two days early. Here I was though, a non-believer standing in a cave elbow to elbow with a crowd of Gentiles.

Once the disciple guy finished his little speech, Jesus entered the stage, cave left. I'd expected him to be the typical, distorted white version of Jesus from my childhood, or maybe even the Mel Gibson version from that terrible movie about torturing Jesus. But never in my wildest dreams had I envisioned a young hippy fella so h-o-t, *hot*. Dear God! With long dirty-blond hair, blue eyes, and a beard, he was a *Legends of the Falls* version of Brad Pitt. Having been a raft guide and ski instructor for most of my twenties, I'd always dated rugged, mountain-man types. Since moving to New York City a few years earlier, though, I hadn't been able to find such earthy-type guys. Until now.

After we listened to Jesus' painfully long monologue about cannibalism, ate our tiny crackers, and downed our shots of grape juice, Jesus finished the show by coming out into the crowd and touching people. He made it a point to lay his hand on all 50 of us saying, "Bless you my child" to adults and children alike. While I knew he wasn't Jesus-Jesus, only the actor playing Jesus, I couldn't help but catch the Jesus fever in the cave, now looking at him almost as a force larger than life.

When it became my turn to get touched, I was a nervous wreck. I'm sure I must have looked like someone straight out of a snake-slinging tent revival since my knees buckled the moment his strong manly hand connected with the spaghetti straps on my shoulder. Blood instantly rushed to my neck and checks, making me blush, and goose bumps popped up all over my arms. Unfortunately, our little moment together was ruined by the sound of my empty wooden shot glass hitting the floor. My poor hand just couldn't concentrate on holding it anymore. When I came back up from retrieving the shot glass, Jesus had already moved on to touching the kid beside me.

I couldn't figure out what in Jesus' name was happening to me. It's not like I was looking for God. I'd already found a new one years ago, one that didn't create a hell or send people like me to it just because we once stole a thousand dollars worth of merchandise from Disney World as a teenager. I honestly didn't care about this Jesus guy or the Bible, and yet here I was falling under his Christian spell.

Just as I was finally starting to pull myself together, Jesus came up from behind and touched me. AGAIN! Now, I don't mean to brag, but I'm the only one in that entire cave who got touched more than once. Not even the children in front of me or the two women beside me in wheelchairs got it twice. After it was all over, I went to follow him out of the cave, but I was told Jesus had to go "pray in the gardens now" (i.e. costume change in the green room). The people around me chanted "Thank you Jesus! *Thank you Jesus!*" over and over as we were escorted out another door by the pharaoh-looking guy who'd dealt out the crackers. I know this is a bit of a stretch, but at the time, part of me thought perhaps this Jesus dude had been flirting with me. He was just a man after all, and men can't help themselves sometimes.

Now that I had the Jesus fever, I was on a mission to see as much of him as possible. I went to several shows, including "The Women Who Loved Jesus." It only seemed appropriate. The stars of this show included his mom, a pissed-off hooker, some woman who was almost stoned to death by a crowd of angry men, and a lady who'd been bleeding for twelve years due to some strange, unexplained disease. You'd think after all my training I would have known my Bible stories a little better, but I was totally lost for the entire show.

If I hadn't been there to see Jesus, my feminist self would have been highly insulted by the content. One pathetic woman after another gave a long-winded speech about how no man cared about her. Then, like a superhero, Jesus would swoop in, she'd cry, he'd save the day, they'd embrace, then she'd give another speech after he left about how obsessed she was with him. They all said phrases like "I've never loved anyone the way I love *that* man," and "I think I love him in a...*different* way," or my personal favorite, "No man has ever touched me in *that* way."

Whenever Jesus wasn't saving some damsel in distress, he was hanging out in the streets of Jerusalem with his homies. Like John Travolta's character in *Grease*, he was the guy every man wanted to be and the hunk every woman wanted to screw. Things took a turn for the worse, however, when out of nowhere a bunch of Roman guards ran on stage and started flogging their hero. At the end of the show an announcer came over the intercom and told us not to miss the follow-up grand finale called "The Passion of the Christ" outside in 20 minutes.

Given the sexual overtones in this last show, one might assume "The Passion of the Christ" was going to be some sort of soft porn, but I had a sneaky feeling it would be a live version of that awful Mel Gibson flick. I usually have a pretty weak stomach, but I couldn't get enough of Hot Jesus.

After all 2,000 of us were herded outside and situated behind ropes like kids awaiting a Fourth of July parade, Jesus came out into a crowd wearing a white robe and hippy sandals. Sweaty, with a bad case of bed head, his mood was somber as he walked around giving another one of his long-winded speeches. Afterward, a group of Roman guards tackled him to the ground. They were pretty hot themselves, each wearing gold-plated six-pack covers and flowing skirts that showed off their soccer legs.

They dragged Jesus over to some fake rocks, where Satan awaited him. Sporting a black robe with a hood, like a character out of a Harry Potter novel, Satan now had his chance to make a speech. Everyone boooo-ed of course, which pleased him greatly.

Once the guards ripped off Jesus' robe, leaving him in an ancient Depends diaper, they bound his hands to a wooden post with rope. If I didn't know better, I would have thought this was some sort of old-timey S&M porno. Each time a whip hit his back, the loudspeakers belted a "crack" sound and fake blood magically appeared. With every lash, Jesus violently arched his back and moaned,

sometimes even making the O-face. This amused Satan,
who laughed hysterically like he was at a taping of *Saturday Night Live.*

When they were done with the whipping part, the
hot guards, now sweaty and jacked-up on testosterone,
dragged Jesus out into the audience and kicked him in
the kidneys repeatedly. By this point in time, my emotions
were all over the place, ranging from disgust at a place that
would let little kids watch such violence, to fear over how
unfazed the crowd was by this insanity. Then Jesus landed
on all fours on the ground in front of me, covered in blood
and sweat and so scantily clad I could almost see his junk
through that diaper. I soon realized I was, more than anything, unbelievably horny.

But you would be too if you were a single 32-year-old
woman who hadn't had sex, much less been kissed or even
touched by a man, in a year and a half. The baby-making
organs of a woman in her sexual prime will latch onto
anything that seems promising, even the Son of God.

It's not that I am a celibate prude. Quite the opposite in
fact. I was prone to the addictive feast-or-famine approach
to life—the one where people like me oftentimes take a
good thing too far and turn it into a bad thing. After my
last binge a couple years ago, I'd decided to cage the little
feline for a while. It's been pretty easy to abstain…until
this Jesus guy showed up.

No wonder I reacted so strongly to Jesus touching me
in the cave. Maybe it hadn't been a spiritual experience
at all—just a sexual one. And that tent revival reaction
of mine was probably just Jesus jolting awake hormones
that'd been on snooze for too long. After the touching
incident, the whipping, and now, here in front of me, a
sweaty, handsome hippie with the body of a swimmer
bent over doggy-style, my inner tiger smelled blood and
desperately wanted out of her cage.

There wasn't much I could do with all this arousal other than continue to watch and take some pictures. Eventually the guards put a thorny crown on his head and made him carry a log, all the while continuing to beat him. I couldn't believe he just kept taking it like a man, never giving up.

Once he was up on the cross, the guards pounded huge spikes through his hands and feet. (The special effects at Holy Land were some of the best I've ever seen, by the way.) They let the poor guy hang up there for quite a while, which was kind of boring to watch until one guard gave him a sponge bath and another speared Jesus in the gut. I must say, even nailed to a cross, the guy looked hot. And that six-pack! I've never been a fan of buff guys, but Jesus had one of those lean-yet-toned figures I always fell for. Sure, I felt bad staring at him "that way" while the people around me cried, but I couldn't help it. This was the first near-naked man I'd been around in ages.

I'm sure you know what happened next. He died. The guards took a hammer to his hands and feet to get the nails out, lowered his perfect body down from the cross, then wrapped him in a white sheet and carried him through the crowd down to a tomb. Satan made a victory speech, and again, the crowd booed.

After the tomb exploded, Jesus appeared again, only this time he had a wardrobe change. All cleaned-up now, he wore a white flowing nightgown, gave another speech, thanked his dad, then held up a set of enormous golden keys in front of the crowd. Anyone who wanted keys to his place, he said, they were there for the taking. Hells yeah I wanted keys to his place! If only he wasn't speaking metaphorically.

All of a sudden, a bunch of angels dressed in white-and-gold disco outfits gathered around him and started twirling, like dancers at a Grateful Dead show. Their gold, sparkly wings fluttered and made cool designs, a visual routine that would have blown the mind of anyone on acid.

We were told to follow the angels to heaven, so all 2,000 of us walked about 50 yards away to a gold-and-white amphitheater, where we were met by even more dancing angels. After about ten minutes, Jesus finally showed up, casually late to his own party, only now he wore a non-thorny crown and a king's robe. As he walked down the aisles, people held their right hands up and screamed "Praise Jesus!" again and again.

Not only was the train of his robe longer than Princess Diana's wedding gown, but he had the aura of a real king. While I've never actually dated a guy with money, I'm still just as much of a sucker as any woman for a handsome man with power and loads of cash. And don't forget fame. He wasn't just the most popular man at Holy Land; he was the most famous person in the *world*. Even more so than Brad Pitt.

Satan made one more appearance, but Jesus had the upper hand now. He threw Satan on the ground by pointing his staff at him and using his superpowers. Two disco angels picked Satan up off the ground and lassoed him with a gold rope before escorting him out of Heaven, once and for all.

As the crowd continued to cheer, and Jesus reveled in his glory, I started to wonder if maybe I had a shot at hooking up with him after the show. I mean, I *was* on vacation and that was usually the only time I ever hooked up with cute guys. Even though I wasn't the prettiest woman at Holy Land, the odds were definitely in my favor. There was absolutely no competition—most good, Christian women wouldn't even consider banging the Holy Spirit. And certainly not in the backseat of a car or in a public restroom like me.

After the show was over, I went looking for Hot Jesus, but he was nowhere to be found. I was willing at this point to even settle for one of the hot Roman guards, but they must have made a dash for the green room too. After wandering around, looking for *any* guy in a costume, I finally gave up on Holy Land and left. Defeated.

Back in NYC, I started noticing a dramatic change in my body. I'd be on a crowded subway or waiting in an hour-long line at Trader Joe's when, all of a sudden, I'd have that knee-buckling experience if a man so much as brushed up against me. These were not good-looking men, or men I'd even consider hooking up with. They were still men though, and I was a single, horny woman in her thirties who still hadn't been touched by anyone in almost two years, except for Jesus of course. Being a hormonal landmine of sorts, I knew I needed to do something.

One day, as if by divine intervention, a kid next to me on the subway grabbed my leg. For the entire subway ride he made sure he always had a hand on someone, if not me or his mom, then another adult close by. It occurred to me at that moment that perhaps I wasn't a horn-ball or a sex-crazed psycho, but rather a human being who just needed to be touched. The need to have physical contact with another human being doesn't go away just because we grow into adults. In fact, once I thought about it, I bet half the men I'd hooked up with in the past had been out of a dire need be hugged.

I knew then and there that I had to find another way to survive in such a dark, lonely city like New York, lest I settle for a boyfriend who's bad for me. So thanks to Jesus, I do what I think any smart single woman ought to do. I pay someone to touch me. Twice a month, I treat myself to a massage. Until, that is, I meet a guy as nice and cute as Hot Jesus.

★

Melanie Hamlett is a writer, comedian, adventurer, and three-time Moth Storyslam winner who's based out of Los Angeles, New Mexico, and New York City, when she's not sleeping on couches or in a tent around the world, or in her truck traveling across America. She's been featured in multiple podcasts, including the Risk! podcast five times, has been published in Marie Claire, Nerve.com, *and the book* Leave the Lipstick, Take the Iguana *(in which this story first appeared). She can be seen performing all over New York City and Los Angeles at places like The Upright Citizens Brigade and The Moth. She's also a frequent monologist for the hit show,* Assscat. *She tells picture-stories about her travels as a wandering narcoleptic at melaniehamlett.com. She's represented by literary agent, Scott Mendel.*

Acknowledgments

THANK YOU TO MY COVER MODELS IN WADI RUM, JORDAN: Chela Lewis, Mike Quigley, Christopher Campbell, Beth Mercer, Samantha Sarafinchan, Leslie Belson, David Zundel, and Gabrielle Broche. And thanks to the readers and experts who answered my incessant questions: Stephen Dennis, Kevin Wrycraft, Snad, Malc, Rigel, Mechelle & Dave Mosher, Michelle Campbell, Doug Milburn, Kimmy Beach and the Dr. of grammar—Gary Buslik. Dear Lavinia Spalding: forward dirty stories my way anytime, and thanks for the ones you flushed my way for this. Thank you to Travelers' Tales, especially James and Sean O'Reilly (see Introduction). Also thanks to my Facebook friends for answering my various surveys about how you read anthologies and how to choose a penis gourd.

About the Editor

KIRSTEN KOZA IS A HUMORIST, JOURNALIST, ADVENTURER, expedition organizer, and the author of *Lost in Moscow: A Brat in the USSR*. She's a contributor to Travelers' Tales anthologies, and her stories "Chasing Tornadoes" and "Mare's Milk, Mountain Bikes, Meteors & Mammaries; a Nipply Night in Nomad's Land" are in *The Best Women's Travel Writing*, volumes 8 and 9. And her misadventure "Easter Island: The Chilean with the Brazilian" is in *Leave the Lipstick, Take the Iguana*.

She's a journalist at *TheBlot Magazine* (Wall St., New York) and covers topics such as cannibalism, bullfighting, dildos, Putin, gluten, twisted travel, tropical diseases, gross food, and outrageous world politics.

Kirsten also leads writing, photography, and eating expeditions around the world for Writers' Expeditions (www.kirstenkoza.com). She received a B.A. in Theater from Dalhousie University (Canada) and completed the Post Grad program at East 15 Acting School (London, England).